IN SEARCH OF GOD
One Soul Many Gods

IN SEARCH OF GOD
One Soul Many Gods

Prof Dr B B Puri

MD PUBLICATIONS PVT LTD
NEW DELHI
www.mdppl.com

"The views expressed in this book are strictly personal and do not reflect anybody's opinion."

Published by :

MD Publications Pvt Ltd
"MD House", 11, Darya Ganj,
New Delhi - 110 002
Phone : +91-11-4535 5555
E-mail (orders): order@mdppl.com
Website: www.mdppl.com

ISBN: 978-81-7533-366-6

Published and Printed by Mr. Pranav Gupta on behalf of **MD Publications Pvt Ltd** at Mohit Enterprises, Delhi.

Prof. Puri enjoying the elements of nature

This Compilation is Dedicated to Lord Shri Krishna

Sanskrit Shloka:

Om ajnana-timirandhasya jnananjana-salakaya
Caksur unmilitam yena tasmai sri-gurave namah

Meaning : "I was born in the darkest ignorance, and my spiritual master opened my eyes with the torch of knowledge. I offer my respectful obeisances unto Him.

CONTENTS

Dr. Priya Ranjan Trivedi
Chancellor, The Global Open University Nagaland
President, Confederation of Indian Universities
Chairman, Indian Institute of Ecology and Environment
President, World Institution Building Programme

Corporate Office :
A 14-15-16, Paryavaran Complex
New Delhi - 110030, India
Website : www.prtrivedi.com
Email : ecology@ecology.edu
Mobile : +91-9818822127
Fax : +91-11-29533514

FOREWORD

It gives me great pleasure to write this foreword to Prof. Dr. B.B. Puri's work on "**In Search of God:** One Soul Many Gods".

Prof. Puri has done a deep study into the relationship between the Vedic Culture, ancient Indian environment and the resultant recipe for peaceful living among the different religions of the world, through the ultimate healing power of love.

Prof. Puri has drawn extensively from the Vedas, Upanishad and the Bhagavad-Gita.

Prof. Puri in his book has discussedVedantic thoughts, ongoing research in the field of humanity and world peace, understanding and respect of other religions in the universe to live in harmony and peace.

This book is especially dealing with the vast experience and knowledge from the learned Author. Prof. Puri conveys in this book the messages through the different chapters on a variety of topics including recarnation and the nature of the soul in relationship with God.

The Author further explains the destiny and the true purpose in life, inner peace with the same soul and many Gods.

The different religions existing in this planet Earth, promises us to show the path to enlightenment which is a blissful state of consciousness. To achieve this state of consciousness, one needs to make a journey within the self soul and the supreme soul paramatma and feel that we are the supreme soul as explained by the Author.

I commend this book not only to the general readers but others in spiritual practice.

I wish Prof. Dr. B.B. Puri a grand success in this and all other future endeavors.

Dr. Priya Ranjan Trivedi
Chancellor, The Global Open University

Letter to Readers

My Dear Divine Soul,

This book is specially for you. The fact that you are reading this book indicates that you want to live a fulfilling, peaceful and spiritual life and enjoy every moment of your richer life.

May this book guide your life with inspiration, guidance spiritual comfort and wisdom. This book will help you achieve new goals, develop a better sense and purpose of life, and generate many new ideas about self, future and guarantee a life time success.

May you be uplifted and inspiration to follow the divine path every minute, every moment and everyday. This book is not meant for gulping the whole book down in one reading. It should be read carefully and understood.

The purpose of this book is to help you in creating an action plan for the rest of your life.

With Love and Blessing, in the service of a Healthy and Peace loving Nation.

Prof Dr B B Puri

ACKNOWLEDGEMENT

Whatever I learn from the different religious societies, spiritual leaders and my experience, over the last 50 years, I have tried to share my experience and explain the same in this book. More over I have tried to express the true knowledge that I learnt and understood from Bhagavad Gita, I therefore have decided to pen down my experience with the aid of vedic knowledge.

My all other previous books are a practical guide to attain the art of blissful living with the help of the spiritual laws of vedic knowledge and drive the benefit through the Ageless Mind within the Life Before Death.

I wish to express my heartfelt thanks to my readers and friends for the wholehearted support and inspiration given to me for writing this book.

My gratitude to Dr. P.R. Trivedi, Chancellor, The Global Open University, Nagaland for writing a very encouraging Foreword for this book.

I am thankful to Mr. R. K. Kataria for taking special pain in final editing of this book and Mr. Raman Mehta for his personal encouragement in this project, my blessing to Ms. Sushma for taking special pain in computer typing & setting the manuscript.

I wish to express my sincere thanks to Mr. Pranav Gupta, Director, MD Publications Pvt Ltd, New Delhi for giving personal attention in the production of this book.

I hope that the learning experience and practical tips which I have accumulated over the past 50 years would help you in opening your mind to rediscover your inner self, to investigate, analyse and realize the very essence of life.

Living a contented life is an art, a skill, and a technique which all of us need to learn and master in order to achieve mental peace and harmony.

This book may help you in creating and maintaining a proper balance between body, mind, soul, intellect and a good positive environment around you.

The tips given in the various chapters offer a practical way of life which satisfies your spiritual needs leading to mental peace along with material prosperity.

Your very self is an ocean with a fortune of undiscovered spiritual life and unbounded love deep inside you that you can offer to others. Your mind is so powerful that you can create an environment of your own choice to surround you.

May this book enlighten your intellect and environment, so that you can enjoy healthy, peaceful and comfortable living within the Laws of Nature.

Last, but not the least, I offer my sincere thanks to all my clients, students, staff and faculty, of Vastu Research Centre,(VRC) Zoroastrian College (Mumbai), Board of Trustee, Research Institute of Vedic Culture,(RIVC) World Academy of Spiritual Science,(WASS), Geriatric Society of India, and The Indian Institute of Building Technologies (IIBT), New Delhi for their cooperation and full support.

Prof Dr B B Puri

PREFACE

After my 80 years of age, learning and experience gained, I have taken courage and attempted to start writing this book as my small contribution to the ongoing research in the field of humanity and world peace, understanding and respect of other religions to live in harmony and peace.

This book is dealing especially with my experiences and knowledge that I have gained from the different spiritual master's around the world spread across the different religions, before birth, life before death, and life after death.

Every word that you will be reading in this book are strictly personal views and do not reflect any body's opinions. As this subject is so delicate, I like to clear that, my mission and aim is to spread peace, harmony and understanding in the universe, and not to hurt anybody's feeling.

I respect all religions alike and have tried to convey the messages through the different chapters of this book. A variety of topics including reincarnation and the nature of the soul, destiny and your true purpose in life, inner peace, healthy mind, body & soul, how to transform your life, your relationships with your family, society and your Nation with the different religions of the world and your self, through the ultimate healing power of love.

Life goes beyond our five senses. Be receptive to new knowledge (gayan) and with new experiences. Our task is to learn, to become same soul (God- like) through knowledge.

I hope that if I can spread, peace & harmony with the effect of this book, it will be more beneficial to the world, than anything that I can do on an individual basis in my life. So far I have already delivered my best - selling following book's apart from the other Technical paper & books to my credit.

- **Life before Death**
- **Ageless Mind**
- **The Art of blissful living**
- **Vastu Science for 21st century to enjoy the gift of nature**
- **Vedic Architecture and Art of Living**

My concluding personal view is "religion promises you to show the path to enlightenment which is a blissful state of consciousness. To achieve this state of consciousness, one needs to make a journey within the self (Atma) soul and the supreme soul parmatma, and that you are the supreme self".

We are a multi - religious society and that is our strength. The source of creation from the nature, by the nature or God is functioning within or from your five senses, you can feel that the God is within you. The question is whether you can see the God or not. The spiritual person can feel it within himself and within every thing and also around every movement. When you say God, or soul we are talking about the basis of physical creation. This dimension cannot be perceived through our five senses. Yes we can achieve through our good karma.

Karma is of many kinds, different layers and dimensions, I will discuss through the different chapters of this book.

All over the world with the sole purpose of guiding human beings to carry out their routine in the best possible and welfare manner under any prevailing circumstances.

But if we choose conscience, it is in our hands to change the path and take the country to a place that we are happy and proud to be in.

The rise of the conscience does not need a specific time. It is within our capacity to allow this to happen. Religion, spiritualism, morality, faith, truth, belief are just words. We give them power in return, these empower us.

Humanity means loving all human beings in the same way as we love ourselves.

Whether they are black or white, healthy or sick, rich or poor, we must love everyone because they are all part of the same universal soul like us. Soul originates from one universal soul or Paramatma just like all colors emanate from a single source of white light. Even though our bodies may be different, our souls are alike, our soul is a silent witness of our actions and thoughts. As God is everywhere, God is like gravity, we cannot see it, cannot touch it, but we know it is abstract, even if it is there, God is not gravity. God is much more above that even though we cannot see God, he is present every where, throughout this universe there is not a Single space or void where God is not present. It is up to us to tune into that signal that God is there. It is like T.V. signal or mobile signal going through us, through everywhere, through space, but we must know how to tune the proper signal and connect the require No's.

Meditation is the way that gives us the path just like every religion has different paths to the same goal, which we call in Hinduism - Brahma or Parmatma, in Islam - Allah, in Christianity - God.

It is possible that we create positive, powerful thoughts in every situation. It requires understanding the functions and effects of thought, process and the practice of Rajyoge Meditation.

Rajyoge Meditation is exploring and experiencing our enormous inner power of mind. It should be noted that neither the brain thinks nor the heart feels but it is the mind which is capable of thinking and feeling. So we should regularly clean our mind from time to time.

The process of clearing the mind is the watching, checking and deleting the unwanted, harmful thoughts. The ability of such mind clearing is found by Rajyoge Meditation which means a connection between the soul and the supreme soul who is the source of all divine powers.

In 21st Century we are too busy in looking after only the garden of materialistic gains. We have neglected the garden of spirituality which is the storehouse of peace, love, inner power, happiness etc. Inner power is already within us. We need to start saving and using it when needed. Economy of thought is developing our inner power we should save our thought energy everyday. As we are conscious of saving petrol, water, electricity etc., we must practice to save our positive invaluable treasure of thought energy. But in this fast modern world of 21st century, practical scenario is such that we waste or lose our precious thoughts, energy, every now and then in small matter's even in a little situation by resisting them. This process of losing thought positive energy goes on for the whole life starting from childhood to old age.

The only remedy of this life - long tragedy is either change the situation or accept the situation. Do not deplete your positive thought energy in continuously resisting the situation which are not in your control.

Prof Dr B B Puri
Author

1

In Search of God

One Soul Many Gods

Since my childhood, I was fascinated to find out in search of God, and wanted to know where is the God? How he looks like ? Where he stays ? How can I reach him? And How to meet him?

I was born and brought up in British Raj. Those days the Britishers had more influence of their culture on us. So I thought the God exists in the church.

So, I requested my father to take me to church. I still remember we were staying in Golmarket near Governor's House (Now Rashtrapati Bhavan, New Delhi) since my father was serving with Viceroy of India. We stayed six months in winter at New Delhi and six months in summer at Shimla. My father took me to church at Goldakhana near Golmarket.

It was Sunday, I sat on a bench in the prayer hall. The father of the church started prayer, after the prayer was over, all devotees started going out of hall mostly Britishers. I was still sitting on the bench to wait for the God. I asked my father that I came here to meet the God, but where is the God? He gave me smile and replied 'let us go home there I will explain you'.

On reaching home I again put the same question. He tried to pacify me that we can not find the God so early. But my questions remained unanswered.

Next Sunday my father took me to Birla Mandir near our home, which was still under construction. He showed me so many murties (idols) of Gods and Goddesses. It was Arti (prayer) time in the evening. The priest (pujari) started arti one by one to all the murties. Started from Shree Laxmi - Narayan, then Durga Maa, then Lord Shiva and Parvati, then Hanuman ji. Then Shri Ram - Sita ji and then Shri Radhe Krishna ji. I asked my father out of so many God's. Who is the real God? My father replied, my son all are real God and Godesses. My father further told me that I will show you more Gods.

He took me to adjoining Temple of Kalibari, but on way he showed me Ganapathi Lord Ganesha, then Goutam Buddha, and Maa Kali-Durga and Devi Saraswati and Mother Laxmi (I went to search for a God). I was very excited to see so many Gods. But at the same time I was confused in my little mind; So many different Questions came to my mind.

I went on putting questions to my father to clarify my mind and tell me more about the each God and Goddess. He told me so many stories, but finally he said that your mother believes in Sanatan Dharma so, she will tell you more in detail, as I believe in Aryasamaj, I do not believe in God's murties Puja (Prayer). Instead of getting answer to my question, I was further eager to know what is difference between Sanatan Dharma and Aryasamaj, is it two different branches of Hindu Dharma? I insisted my father to please clarify and tell me more in detail.

Next Sunday morning my father took me to Aryasamaj Mandir, where lots of people sat around Havan Kund, where fire was burning and chanting of ved mantras was going on and also samagri was put into the fire after each mantra. Being a small child I was not so competent to put more questions I don't understand the difference between the two Temples, Sanatan Dharma mandir and Aryasamaj mandir. Both are different in their Philosophy.

I repeatedly asked my question to my mother, I noticed that my mother offered prayer every morning and evening, she regularly went to mandir (temple) with Puja thali, (a decorated plate with some fresh flowers, Agarbati Dhoop and a deepak) and on her return from temple she brought some sweets, and distributed among all family members saying please take prasad. (Blessing of God)

Both my father and mother were very religious, my father regularly went to Aryasamaj mandir on Sunday morning, and my mother went to temple every morning, but both my father and mother respected each other, some time she took us to Aryasamaj with all our family and every Sunday all our family members alongwith our father visited temple together. Both my father and mother were so regular that they kept the names of all their children in the name of religions. May be my Grandfather put my father's name Kishan Chand and mother name Ram Payrey.

I have two elder brothers named Om Prakash, and Ved Rathan, one sister named Prem Kumari, myself Bharat Bhushan.

My father and mother believed in two different religions out of Hindu Religious Aryasamaj and Sanatan Dharma, but both had a deep understanding and respect for each other's religion.

They together celebrated all the religious ceremonies and festivals, not only for our Hindu's festivals but also the festivals of all religions such as Christianity, X-Mas, Islamic, Sikhism, Jainism and Buddhism, those were the religious ceremonies in British Rules and we celebrated together with our neighbours and friends.

Shimla is about 7,000 feet height in Himalaya north of India. It was summer, nice weather in Shimla. In Shimla there were two Main shopping Bazars, The Mall, only for Britishers, (Indian were not allowed) and other for Indians named as Lower Bazar. Our colony was surrounded with lots of green pine trees, situated on the peak of the hill.

The function was well organized in our house, well decorated by flags made out of thin multicolor papers and fresh flowers.

I still remember that my parents had organized a very big function in our house. I was about five and a half or six year of age, we were staying in British Government colony in Shimla.

The function was called YOGEPAVITRA (the janeou thread ceremony) for our three brothers. The function was attended and witnessed by our relatives, neighbours, friends and few British officers' with their wives.

We all three brothers had to wear only a orange color dhoti on our lower part of our body, and sit around a holifire (Havan Kund).

Vedic Mantras were chanted by four priests (pujaris) for few hours. After that priests put tilak on our forehead and gave each of us a sacred thread made out of three cotton threads to wear across our body. The priest (Pujari ji) explained in brief the importance of these threads called Janeou made out of three cotton threads, to be worn for rest of our life.

The important meaning of each thread is that we are born in this Earth planet with the blessing of our parents, and develop our five senses with the blessing of our teacher (guru) and spend our life in our society with dignity.

The importance of first thread is to repay our gratitude towards our parents, the second thread represents the gratitude towards our teachers (Guru) and the third thread represents that we have to repay our gratitude towards our society / towards our country.

They further told us that we must remember and be grateful, and give highest respect to first our Parents who gave birth to us and second highest respect to our Guru (teacher) who gave us Knowledge (Gyan) and third to our society, for which the God has sent us on this planet Earth.

After the ceremony we were told to take the blessings first from our parents, second from the priests (Pujari ji) who were performing the Puja and third from all guests present there. I remember there were British Muhammadans, sikh families, and Jain families who gave their respected blessings to us. In the end of ceremony we all had lunch together, which in Hindu philosophy is called PRITIBHOJ, meaning eating together the healthy food, with the healthy people, in the healthy society.

Time passes but my eagerness in search of the God was more established in my young mind. I still remember that the next day my school was closed as holiday for an Id festival.

Our next door neighbour was a very nice friendly Muhammadan Family. Their son was of my age, and in the morning he informed me that they were going to Jama-masjid Chandni-chowk for Id prayer, and after returning they will celebrate Id with eating food together with special dish sweet 'semeya'. I asked him if I can also join them to Jama-masjid, they agreed and took me with them.

They hired a Tongha (horse and cart) to go to Chandni-chowk Jama-masjid. Inside the Jama-Masjid I saw all people sitting in discipline lines and praying together. But my eyes were looking for God. I found no statue or Idol of any God there, except an elderly respected person with white beard leading the prayer.

After the Id prayer everyone present there was greeting

and hugging each other. It was very affectionate site to see that how everyone was loving and respecting each other. I was very much impressed with the sight. After coming back home, we all celebrated Id by eating together sweet (semeya), made of Milk.

Time passed on and my heaps of questions and confusion about where I can find God and my search to find God in my mind started disturbing me.

One fine morning I saw a procession of sikhs all wearing turbans and chanting Kirtan. I was told that this day was the birthday of Shri Guru Gobind Singh ji. So the sikhs committee was celebrating it. I insisted my father to take me to Gurdwara Rakab ganj. It was a holiday and my father took me to Gurdwara Rakab Ganj.

Before entering the prayer hall, my father covered our heads with hankies, we went inside the main hall where some sikh Granthy was singing and chanting the Gurbani next to Shri Guru Granth Sahib the Holy book. But my little eyes' were in search of God. No one was there to tell me where I can find my God.

Time passed, the more I grew, the more I wanted to know about the different religions and God.

In my school, the history was my most favourite subject where I learned about the Hindu period, the Mughal period, and the British period, their rulers and the religion. As the time slowly passed, I started knowing the different religions, Castes and different believers in God. But my search for God was becoming more difficult and confused.

My mother's sister (Massi Ji) staying in Jammu (J and K) visited us in New Delhi on her way to Haridwar and Rishikesh. I insisted Massi ji to take me with her to Haridwar and Rishikesh. She agreed and my parents happily sent me with her.

We stayed in Haridwar and Rishikesh for about 15 days,

where I met so many rishis, munis and saints. I found the opportunity to clear my mind about where I can find my God. So many had advised me that this is not the age to find answers to such questions. Some had tried to show me the different idols of God and Godess, that they are our God. The more I knew about Hindu Dharma (Religion) the more I was confused.

One day when we were in Rishikesh, staying in Dharamsala, I met a saint who explained me "**that, my little son, God is within you. The God is within every one inside like Atma (Soul) that is connected with parama-atma and our Atma (Soul) again merges after our death with parama-atma. That we call parmatma, the God.**"

He further explained that the Atma called Soul is universal and secular, and is in every human being. We are alive, living or breathing only when our soul is within our body. When the soul detaches from our body, then the soul or body become two different parts. The soul merges with the supreme soul called parmatma God and the existing body becomes breathless and we call it a dead body or death.

At that time it was very difficult for me to understand this philosophy, but with the passage of time, knowledge, education, meeting different people, around the world, I learned a lot and discovered new things after meeting with the different spiritual leaders of different Religions and also my own study, and research from the Vedas, Upanishad, Ramayan and Bhagwat Gita motivated me to write this book.

All of the religions have developed from time-to-time in various places of the world with the sole purpose of guiding human beings to carry-out their routine within themselves and for the harmony of their society in the best possible and welfare manner under any prevailing circumstances.

In my early age many questions were established in my young mind. Why there are so many Gods and religions in our society and in one religion there are so many Gods and Godess. The religion is also further deviled into many parts like Hinduism, Sanatan Dharama (with many Gods and Godesses). In Aryasamaj they don't worship God, and in Islam, Suni and Shia, in Jainism, Degamber and Swetamber etc.

The more I wanted to know about the religion and also in search of God, the more complicated subject I started feeling, but my questions contained more and more inquires without getting any answer to my satisfaction.

Muni Sushil Kumar Ji, a Jain priest founded an International society, called World Fellowship of Religion. Under the chairmanship of Muni Sushil Kumar ji, I was appointed as Secretary General for this society. Under this society we organized many national and international seminars / conferences. During this period I had the opportunity to meet many World Spiritual Leaders. To know more closely and in depth about different Religions from the different Saints and Spiritual Leaders, and also about the concept of God, I came to understand the philosophy of religion that:

PATHS AND FAITHS ARE DIFFERENT
BUT THE GOD IS ONE,

To understand this philosophy one must study in depth and in full devotion.

2

All Religions as I Learn

HINDUISM

Hinduism is Sanatana Dharma. It means eternal law.

Philosophy of Dharma is Righteousness, Love Service, Austerity, Simplicity and Faith in the Divine Lord.

Artha (money) is the means of living. It is not the aim. Dharma precedes Artha. To earn money in righteous way without hurting others, without cheating others, without grabbing others, means of livelihood and possession.

Kama denotes love and lust. Love for all is the righteous way of love, satisfies natural instinct of Kama (lust) for ongoing creation. Lust is to be limited. So Righteousness (dharma) precedes artha (money) and kama (lust & love).

Moksha means liberation. Human body is manifestation of infinite parambrahma. In duality, as human being, we enjoy Brahma (Supreme Lord). In non-duality a person is merged with the Lord. Liberation means to realize this ultimate truth and merge in the Lord while following the path of Dharma, Love and Service.

Scriptures of Hinduism are based on Sruti (revealed) and Smriti (remembered). Main scriptures are four Vedas, Rgved (ऋगवेद), Yajurved (यजुर्वेद), Saamved (सामवेद) and Atharwaved (अथर्ववेद). Upanishads, Puranas, Mahabharata, Ramayana, The Bhagwat Gita a treatise from the Mahabharata spoken by Lord Krishna to Arjun is the essence of the teaching of Vedas.

Hinduism believes in "creation, sustenance and destruction of world by Divine Lord". Reincarnation based on Karma Yoga, Rajas Yoga, Bhakti Yoga and Gyan Yoga is the teaching of Lord Krishna.

The syllable Om represents Parambrahma. Om is the divine sound at the time of creation of the world when the world was void.

Scriptures give insight and philosophical teaching to the living world and how to realize the ultimate truth and reality with all happiness in austerity and simplicity.

Max Muller and Josh Woodroffe translated Vedas & Upanishad in English for the knowledge of the world. Enlightened teachers like Sri Tulsidas, Sant Kabir, Sri Sri Aurobindo, Paramhansa Sri Yoginandji, Swami Vivekanand ji, Swami Rama have been awakening the true meaning of existence and love, the magnetic force balance the cosmic creation. Epic Ramayana sways the common masses, influences their devotion to God and establishes the righteousness living and destruction of person/persons who follow the path of unrighteousness.

Hindus believe that there is a spirit Him the sword cannot pierce-him the fire cannot burn-him the water cannot melt-him the air cannot dry.

Like all rivers flowing to sea, all various paths of religions lead to one cosmic/divine power/ God. It is oneness. It is universal oneness.

VARIOUS RELIGIONS

Hinduism

Buddhism

Jainism

Christianity

Islam

Sikhism

Judaism

Taoism

Shintoism

Bahai

Zoroastrian

Bahai Lotus Temple, New Delhi

BUDDHISM

Buddhism had its origin in the teachings of Gautama Buddha of the 5th century before Christianity became the world religion. Buddha saw truth by intuition and realization. He was born in a royal family. Being moved by seeing an old man, a diseased person, a dead body and a sannyasin, he was moved and plunged into deep thought. After 6 years of renouncing everything, desired enlightenment dawned upon him. He preached full forty five years. He is not only the light of Asia but "the light of the world". Swami Vivekananda said, "He was the ideal karmayogi acting without motive, he was the greatest man ever born beyond compare."

Five Precepts: One has to abstain from killing, stealing, adultery, lying and liquor.

Eight Fold Path: Right understanding, thought, speech, action, livelihood, effort, mind fulness and concentration.

Buddha looks equally with a kind heart to all the living being.

Buddhism is not a belief system or an abstract philosophy. It is a way of life, teaching, how to behave and to cultivate qualities. It aims to awaken true nature, the enlightened qualities of a Buddha. The way of Buddha is to know yourself. Enlightenment / Nirvana is natural to human experience. Rational self introspection enables a person to achieve a higher state of discipline and harmony. Mind is intrinsically pure. Within itself it is already peaceful. See the original mind. Train the mind to know the sense impression and not get lost in them. The aim is to make the mind peaceful. There are four noble truths:

1. The existence of suffering. The Pali word is Dukha. The suffering permeates our existence, affecting both our minds and bodies. Happiness occurs, and then disappears often quite quickly.
2. The cause of suffering is desires. We look inside; we discover we are full of desires. External circumstance, are just being blamed by us. We want to be rich and famous. I want to be good. I would like to help alleviate the third world's poverty. These seem to be good ideas. These are still desires and cause us suffering.
3. The cessation of the causes of suffering. It is possible. It is Nirvana. It is eternal.
4. The path that leads to cessation of the cause of suffering-it is a set of guidelines for living in a way that will help liberate us from being driven by our desires and create the causes for us eventually to attain Nirvana.

Buddhism is to practice, to do, not just the usual religious consolations. We must make an effort, salvation lies in our own hands, but we have to work towards it.

In Rabindranath Tagore's novel Ghare Baire (Home & world) the author declares " It was Buddha who conquered the world, not Alexander" for Buddha threw light on something of eternal value".

A Journey to Enlightenment

Gautam Buddha came to Uruvilva (Buddha Gaya) and sat there beneath a Bo-tree, with a vow to attain enlightenment. After six years of hard and severe ascetic life, desired enlightenment dawned upon him and he became Bodhisattva. He realized that "neither my life of luxury in the palace nor my life as an ascetic in the forest is the way to freedom. Overdoing things cannot lead to happiness" He began to eat nourishing food again and regained his strength.

"Awaken yourself" he resolved to find out something which transcends all worldly relationships and pleasures. On full moon day, he sat under the Bodhi tree in deep meditation and said" I will not leave this spot until I find an end to suffering" He realized that a pure unsullied consciousness confers the highest knowledge. True knowledge is delivered from a pure inner consciousness (Antahkarana). He realized the cause of suffering and how to remove it. He became Buddha "The Awakened One". From then on he was called Shakyamuni Buddha. He said about himself' Buddha is the name of the infinite as the sky I Gautama have reached the state, you will reach that too if you struggle for it". Buddha looks equally with a kind heart on all living beings".

"O bhikshus, follow the middle path-keep aloof from both extremes- Mortification is not conducive. Mortifications are painful vain and profitless. To satisfy the necessities of life is not evil. To keep the body in good health is a duty, for otherwise we shall not be able to trim the lamp of wisdom and keep our mind strong and clear.

Lost in the universe: "The first truth is that nothing is lost in the universe. Matter turns into energy, energy turns into matter. We consist of that which is around us. We are the same as everything. If we destroy something around us. We destroy ourselves if we cheat another. We cheat ourselves.

Everything changes: "Buddha said that everything is continuously changing. Life is like a river, flowing on an on, ever changing to meet the sea. As water flows over our hands, changes occur in life, no matter what we do. The key to happiness is being able to appreciate this single truth.

Laws of cause and effect: This is continuous change due to law of cause and effect. The law of cause and effect is known as karma. Good work will reap good results. A kind of seed sown will produce a kind of fruit. If we do evil we will have evil results.

Buddha's emphasis was on purity in vision, purity in thought, purity in speech and purity in action. The spirit of sacrifice is true yajna (religious rite), sacrifice in the means for attaining Nirvana (freedom from the bondage of mundane existence) renunciation means losing both our attachment to those things we like, and our aversion to unpleasant situations and feeling, realizing that none of these things have an inherent ability to make us happy or unhappy".

The five hindrances-Buddha said that five mental states hinder our spiritual progress and perpetuate sufferings. They are

i) sensual desire

ii) ill will

iii) sloth and torpor

iv) Worry and restlessness

v) Confused doubt. Sloth and torpor are best over come by eating less and taking more exercise.

Confused doubt can be overcome by reading and understanding the teachings of Buddha. Worry and restlessness arise from uneasy conscience. By resolving not to do and thinking negative thoughts and actions will lesson worry and restlessness a problem shared is a problem halved.

The Noble Eight path –

These are defined under three categories – wisdom, morality and meditation to be cultivated together.

(1) Right View or understanding belongs to wisdom. We are responsible for our own destiny. We cannot change circumstances or people but can change our reactions to them. Right View will steer us towards Right Action and thereby freedom from suffering.

(2) Right Thought or intention-usually our thoughts are egocentric. These are how best to serve one self. Right thought has three dimensions- renunciation, goodwill and harmlessness. Negative thoughts need to be substituted with

Right thoughts by understanding the Noble Truths and meditation.

(3) Right Speech is about being conscious and aware of what we are saying and doing. Four elements of Right Speech are: -

(a) Abstaining from false speech or lying and cultivating truthful speech

(b) Abstaining from slanderous speech and cultivating speech that promotes friendship and harmony

(c) Abstaining from harsh speech, shouting, insulting or being sarcastic and cultivating courteous and friendly speech.

(d) Abstaining from idle chatter including TV, radio, newspaper etc. telling the truth if possible, is the best course of action. Abstaining from criticizing others.

(4) *Right Action* - is not to hurt others. It includes not killing any living being even self not taking what is not given, not misusing the senses and not using the senses and not using intoxicants.

(5) *Right Livelihood* - making a living in ethical way without harming any living entity.

(6) *Right Effort* - Not trying too hard or too little. If we do not try hard enough, then nothing much will happen and we have merely wasted our time, money and efforts. After trying hard, if success is not there, then learn when to stop. Self training, self control are needed to have right effort and success.

(7) *Right Mindfulness* - the active watchful mind and deep meditation on the realities of life. It includes mindfulness of body, of feeling, of thinking and of the objects of thoughts. Mindfulness grounds the mind firmly in the present, preventing if floating off into nostalgic memories, hopes and fears. It entails watching our thoughts without becoming involved with them.

Right Concentration- is developed by using calm or tranquil abiding meditation and insight meditation. It develops single pointed ness of mind. To stay focus on the subject so chosen. It is developed in stages. Better to develop under guidance of an able teacher.

JAINISM

Lord Mahavir was the 24th Tirthankara or prophet of the Jain religion. His preaching is Ahimsa (Non-Violence), Anekanta (Non-Absolutism) and Aparigarha (Non Possession).

Liberated souls are supreme in this world.

"Do not injure anyone and do good to all that you can. Man has to bear his sorrow all alone. Attachment and aversion are the root causes of karma and karma is originated from delusion".

Dharma is essence. The ten virtues are forgiveness, right faith, right knowledge, right conduct, giving protection to living creatures, supreme forgiveness, humility, straightforwardness, truthfulness, purity, self restraint, austerity, renunciation, detachment, continence.

"Conquer anger by forgiveness, pride by humility, deceit by straightforwardness and greed by contentment."

"Mediate on one's soul after controlling one's diet, posture, sleep and gaining knowledge wholesome and healthy food, in lesser quantity."

"Be free from fear and let others be free from fear"

There should be no color, no taste, no smell, no touch, and no gender. The pure soul is free from the activities of mind, body and speech. It is full of infinite knowledge and perception, firmly established in the self.

CHRISTIANITY

The Christianity is a faith in Jesus Christ; the son of God, the savior. It is centered on the life and teachings of Jesus as presented in the New Testament.

Resurrection of Jesus after three days of his death is the most important event. According to the gospels of Mathew and Luke, Jesus was conceived by the Holy Spirit and born from the Virgin Marry.

Trinity is an essential doctrine of Christianity "Father, son and the holy spirit". God is believed to be infinite. Trinity is also being defined as one God in three persons. Bible is the holy book. It is in two parts (The Old Testament & the New Testament).

Christians assemble for communal worship on Sunday, the day of resurrection. The Cross is one of the most widely recognized symbols in the world.

ISLAM

Arabia about the time of Muhammad's birth in Mecca in AD 570 was in a state of religious unrest. There was urgent need of moral reform. At the age of forty, Muhammed received his first "divine revelation" in the solitude of the mountains near Mecca.

Onward he felt he had a mission in life to the people from moral degradation. He proclaimed himself as the messenger of God to mankind.

He suffered every kind of indignity when he began to denounce the worship of idols and observance of superstitious practices, He migrated to Madina. He sent missionaries to all parts of Arabia and even to neighbouring countries including Egypt and Persia.

Prophet Muhammad's lessons

- Have faith in God.
- Abandoning that which God disapproves.
- Purity and hospitality.
- Free from malice towards anyone.
- To love him who loves God.
- To do unto all men and women as you would wish them to have done unto you.
- Speak the truth.
- Perform what you promise.
- Be chaste.
- Serve humanity-feed the hungry, serve sick.
- Resign to the will of God.
- Acquire riches in lawful manner.
- Love neighbor.
- Hold the oppressor from oppression.
- Who ever does good to you, return the same to him.
- God is merciful. He is gracious. He is pure. He loves the pure.
- Adore God. He sees you.
- God is humble. Be humble.
- God is One. He likes unity.
- One will enter heaven, if one has faith in heart equal to a single grain of mustard seed.

- Faith is a restraint against all violence.
- He who his own self, knows God.
- With knowledge man rises to the heights of goodness and to a noble position.

SIKHISM

Sikhism was founded by the teachings of Guru Nanak Dev and ten successive Sikh gurus in the 15th century in Punjab.

Sikhism has faith in "Waheguru" using the sacred symbol of "Ikonkar", the universal God. Holy scriptures are the Guru Granth Sahib (Adigranth) and Dasam Granth.

Sikhism believes in equality of all humans. God is one, but He has innumerable forms. God is love. God is unity. The same God resides in the temple, in the mosque and outside as well. Spiritual union with God is the ultimate aim of life. They believe in an endless cycle of birth i.e reincarnation.

Sikhism accepted some of the basic doctrines of Hinduism. God is Absolute, All pervading, and external. He is the Creator, the cause of causes. Life is not sinful in its origin. God himself takes human form.

To make His will your own will is the means to achieve Him. Give up to His Supreme will. He cannot be comprehended by reason; one can never have contentment even with the riches of the world. All things are manifestation of His will. Discover untold spiritual riches within yourself. God is the only Doer. Remember Him day and night, so pure is God's name. Whoever obeys God, knows the pleasure of it, it has own heart. God's name is the ocean of peace.

Guru is God like in power as creator, protector and destroyer. In Hinduism "Guru Brahma Guru Bishnu Guru Shiva Guru's God" (Govinda both are standing, whom should I salute first.)

Three essentials for spiritual realization of soul to God- Satguru, Satsang at holy assembly & prayers and Satnaam chanting name of God.

Like other religions Sikhism says, "Conquer your mind for victory over self; victory over self is the victory over the world."

Third Guru Amar Das's son in law Ram Das founded the city of Amritsar the Harmindar Sahib, the holiest city of Sikhs. The 6th guru Har Govindji created "Akal Takht" (the throne of timeless one) serving as the supreme decision making centre of Sikhdom.

Guru Tegh Bahadur was executed by Aurangzeb for helping to protect Hindus. Govind Singh ended the line of human gurus and now the guru granth sahib serves as the eternal guru, with its interpretation vested with the community.

Nanak taught that ritual, religious ceremonies or idol worship is of little use and Sikhs are discouraged from fasting or going on pilgrimages. Gurudwaras are open to all, regardless of religion, background, caste or race.

Guru Nanak's japji

Jap meaning recitation of the divine name to combine all negative thoughts out of the mind.

Sikh's religion does not permit divorce. Khalsa (meaning pure) is the name given by Govind Singh to all Sikhs who have been baptized by taking Ammrit.

Guru Nanak said, "As fragrance abides in the flower, as the reflection is within the mirror so does the lord abide within you."

The ray has merged in the sun, the wave in the sea, the light has merged in the light and man is fulfilled.

Whatever you practice day and night has been written on your forehead. How clear is the path of one who believes in Guru! He lives with honour, with honour he walks straight on the highway.

JUDAISM

Judaism is the 'religion, philosophy, and way of life' of the Jewish people. Originating in the Hebrew Bible (also known as the Tanakh) Judaism is considered by Jews to be the expression of the covnantal relationship which God developed with the Children of Israel.

Judaism is a monotheistic faith as it believes in only One God. Often this God is beyond our ability to comprehend, but God is nevertheless present in our everyday lives. Some connect with God through prayer, others see the divine in the majesty of the natural world, and others may not think about God on a daily basis. Humankind in Judaism is the divine image of God. For this reason every person is equally important and has an infinite potential to do good in the world. People have the free will to make choices in their lives and each of us is responsible for the consequences of those choices. Judaism believes that Jews are uniquely connected and all Jews are part of a global Jewish community.

The Torah is Judaism's most important text which contains stories and commandments that teach about life and death. It contains the 10 Commandments as well as the 613 commandments that all Jews consider to be the most important are:

1. I am the Lord.
2. You shall not recognize the Gods of others in My presence.
3. You shall not take the Name of the Lord, your God in vain.
4. Remember the day of Shabbat to keep it holy.
5. Honor your father and your mother.
6. You shall not murder.
7. You shall not commit adultery.
8. You shall not steal.
9. Do not give false testimony against your neighbor.
10. You shall not covet your fellow's possessions.

TAOISM (DAOISM)

It is the main stream of traditional religion in China. The word Tao (or Dao) translates as the 'path or way' of life. In Chinese religion and philosophy, Tao emphasizes three jewels- 'compassion, moderation, humility.' Taoist thought generally focuses on nature, the relationship between humanity and the cosmos, health and longevity and wuwei (action through inaction) which is considered to produce harmony with the Universe.

Robinet asserts that Taoism is better understood as a way of life than a religion. "Man is a macrocosm for the Universe. The body ties directly into the Chinese five elements, five organs correlate with the five elements, five directions and the seasons. Man may gain knowledge of the Universe by understanding himself. Various rituals, exercise and substance are said to positively attract one's physical and mental health. They are also intended to align one spiritually with cosmic forces or enable ecstatic spiritual journeys.

Some of the essence of Taoism and Hinduism appears to be the same. Lord Krishna told Arjuna, 'Action is inaction and inaction is action.' One of the means to be near Divinity: 'Five elements and five organs are to be regulated.'

SHINTOISM

Shinto is one of the ancient religions of the world. It has originated from Japan. The venerable Daien Shinya Uchida, Director of the Nihonji Temple of Tokyo says: This religion of the ancestors which takes the form of the worship of many Gods... Before the advent of Budhism in Japan, some Hindu Gods and Goddesses had already been integrated in to ancient Shintoism.

The worship of seven divine powers that shower blessings on the Japanese is common.

They are:-

1. *Deikutan* The God of wealth and destiny. He has been taken from India where he is known as Mahakal Shiva.
2. *Bishahonten* Or the Indian Vaishvarnas.
3. *Benjeiten* Goddess of destiny or the Indian Saraswati.
4. *Fukrokui* The God of wealth and longevity from China.
5. *Bibeeso* God of wealth.
6. *Jurojin* God of longevity.
7. *Hotei* God of treasure from China.

Among these Deikokutun (Lord of Death, Shiva), Bishahonten (Vaishvarnam) and Benjeitan (Sarawati) are forms of the Hindu Shiva, Hanuman and Mother Gauri.

In Shinto, a God is called "Kami". The world 'Kami' means a pure, great and extraordinary being having virtues of being infinite, omnipotent and omniscient. The word 'Kami' is used for deities of heaven and earth and also for soul living in cemeteries. Together with this, the world is used or animals, birds, rivers, mountains, etc. All these are fearsome but because of their extra-ordinary powers also worthy of worship. Similarly, Gods of fire, storm and rain are considered fearful and therefore need to be propitiated by worship. Shintoism recognizes two kinds of Gods-deities of nature and deities of man. However, these deities are not spiritual but are like human beings and they are imagined to have the virtues and vices of men. Some deities are supposed to be inhabited by spirits. They live in temples informally and act as bridge between heaven and hell.

Among these deities, the most respected is the sun. But in Shintoism, the sun is not a man but a woman. Perhaps that is because woman has occupied the most important space in Japan from ancient times.

In the modern age, Shintoism can be divided into three types-Jinja Shinto, Kyoha Shinto and Minjoku Shinto.

In Jinja Shinto, God is worshiped in constructed temples that the Japanese call Jinja. This is a branch of Shinto that had its origin in ancient times. Jinja Shinto has played a significant role in Japanese village life and in the unification and organization of Japan as a nation. According to Japanese thinker Ono Sokyo, Shintoism is a religion based on the ancient tradition of Japan. Ameterasu Omi Kami is considered the supreme Goddess and is worshipped as such. Together with this, ancestors are worshipped and prayers are said for the peaceful development of the ancient nation.

Kyoho Shinto is also known as Shuha Shinto. This

religion is centered on thirteen groups organized during the nineteenth century. Among these, each groups or community has office-bearers and organizers. They have organized their communities amongst the people. There are no temples in Kyoha Shinto.

Minjoku Shinto is based on customary belief of the people. These popular beliefs are derived from ancient traditions, rituals and rites emphasizing purity and the Gods and Goddesses worshipped in homes and fields. But these three communities are not separate. They are mutually interlinked.

In ancient times, temples had a role in the Shintoism. Religious rituals and rites were performed in place considered sacred and at the foot of some mountain, on banks of rivers or groves of trees. Later, in order to protect these places from the elements like rain and sun, a small hut began to be erected. Later of these huts they became the prototypes for the temple. With this the concept of Kami began to change. Upto the nineteenth century, agriculture was the main source of livelihood in Japan. Consequently, in ancient Shintoism the major part of worship and prayer is connected with agriculture.

In Shintoism the religious rituals of worship and prayer are not complex. It is enough to dedicate offerings of worship to God to please Him and to repent for one's sins. Ordinary rice, bread, meat, deer, pig or birds are offered to the Gods. Before worship, it is essential to bathe. After bath, it is a customary obligation to put on clean clothes. Any one who is sick or has a wound is prohibited from performing religious rites. Similarly, a person who has performed the funeral rites of some one who died in the family, is disqualified from performing religious rituals.

It is customary to place a mirror, a sword and precious stones in front of the idol in Shintoism. The followers of Shintosm bow in front of them.

Shintoism has also embraced elements of Buddhism. Buddhism entered Japan in the year 538. Initially, the followers of Shinto accepted Lord Buddha as the Kami or God of the neighbouring country, China. Soon the cultured people of Japan began to be influenced by the principles, art and devotional rituals of Buddhism. During the middle ages, from 710 to 784, which are also known as the Nara period, Buddhism became popular as the royal mode of worship. The influence of Shinto, too, remained undiminished and soon an intimate relationship developed between the two traditions. There are said to be three phases in the integration of Shintoism and Buddhism. In the first phase, Kami or the Japanese Gods came to be regarded as the protectors of the Buddha. He, too, began to be worshipped in Buddhist temples. In 749, together with the construction of great Buddha in Todaiji, a temple was constructed nearby for the worship of Kami also. In the second phase it was believed that kamis were primarily the result of ignorance of karma and other related issues. They suffered the pain of birth, death and rebirth, like mortals. To help in their liberation, Kami temples began to be contructed near Buddhist temples and Buddhist teachings began to be recited there.

Towards the end of the eighth century the third phase began when Kami began to be considered the incarnation of the Bodhisattva. Later, the idea took hold that Buddha was the primary form of Kami. Consequently, Buddha began to be established in Shinto temples and the idols of Kami took the form of Buddhist priests. By A.D. 1000, Buddha began to be considered an incarnation of Kami. By A.D. 1100 a special relationship was established between Kami and Bodhisattva. From 1603 to 1867, the administrators of more than half the Shinto shrines were Buddhist bhikshus.

During this time, in the first half of the fifteenth century the priest of the Yoshida temple at Kyoto, Urabe Kanetimo, established Yoshida Shintoism.

Together with Buddhism, the Japanese mind was also impressed by Confucius as a result of which Confucius Shinto religion came into existence. During this period, thirteen sects of Shintoism arose because of the influence of Shintoism, Confucianism, Buddhism, Taoism and other popular beliefs.

The Religious Books of Shintoism

'Kojiki' (the book of ancient writings) and Nihonshoki or Nihonji (the history of Japan) are accepted as the two main religious texts of Shintoism.

BAHÁ'Í FAITH

The Bahá'í Faith was, founded by Bahá'u'lláh in nineteenth-century, emphasizing the spiritual unity of all humankind. In the Bahá'í Faith, religious history is seen to have unfolded through a series of divine messengers. These messengers have included Krishna, Buddha, Zoroaster, Moses, Jesus, Prophet Muhammad among others and most recently the Báb and Bahá'u'lláh. The followers of Bahá'í religion believe:-

- All humanity is one family.
- Women and men are equal.
- All prejudices - racial, religious, national, or economic are destructive and must be eradicated.
- We must investigate truth for ourselves, without preconceptions.
- Science and religion are in harmony.
- Our economic problems are linked to spiritual problems.

- The family and its unity are very important.
- There is one God.
- All major religions come from God.
- World peace is the crying need of our time

History of Bahá'í Faith

Bahá'í is one of the leading Faiths of the world. It is a universal and independent world religion, the doors of whose temples are open to believers of all religions and races. The primary aim of Bahá'í religion is to create a feeling of oneness in all. It believes that Prophet Abraham collected a tribe and united it. Moses had made men one and the Prophet Muhammad a nation. Jesus worked for the purity of the human soul. Every prophet sent by God did his work fully. What remained was the collective purity of the entire human race; the completion of this work is the aim and duty of the Baha'i Faith.

Bahá'í religion is only a century and half old. It was founded in the later half of the 19th century by Mirza Husayn- 'Ali Nuri (1817-1892). People reverently called Him, Baha'u'llah which means the "Glory or Light of God". The forerunner of the Bahá'í Faith, the Báb (1819-1850), whose followers were known as Bábis, had prophesied that a prophet would come among them. It is on the basis of this prophecy that the Bábis regarded Bahá'u'lláh, as the Promised One and they became known as Bahá'ís.

To understand the Bahá'í Faith, it is essential to become familiar with the life of its founder, Bahá'u'lláh. He was born in a prosperous family in Tehran, Irán. His father was Minister at the court of the Shah of Iran. According to the Bahá'í history and Bahá'u'lláh Himself, he never went to any *madarsa* (school) for education. From his childhood, he had an inclination towards spirituality. He himself got initiated into the Bábi teachings when he first heard of the Báb in 1844. Although he never met Báb personally, he was well acquainted with his religious book the Bayán and other Writings through divine intuition.

Bahá'u'lláh declared Himself to be the Promised One on 21st April 1863 in the garden of Najib Pasha (which the Bahá'ís consider to be the Bagh-i-Rizwan or Garden of Paradise), just as Báb had prophesied earlier.

Some months after the exile in Istanbul, Bahá'u'lláh was sent to Edirne (the European part of Turkey) where he openly announced his mission as Prophet of the new Age and wrote letters (called Tablets) to the kings and rulers of his time such as Sultan 'Abdu'l-'Aziz, Nasir'ud-Din Shah, Pope Pius IX, Queen Victoria, Czar Alexander II, Napoleon III, Francis Josef, Kaiser Wilhelm I, acquainting them with his vision of a new World Order and warning of the impending crises that were bound to afflict humanity due to wars, disunity, religious conflicts, economic disparities, and contamination of the earth's atmosphere, *inter alia*. These communications are well documented and are available in the original Persian and Arabic as well as translations into major languages of the world.

Some followers of Bahá'u'lláh at the instigation of his half-brother, Shubih-i-Azal, (later his followers called themselves Azalis) who became jealous caused a lot of suffering and disturbance in the community. As a result some incidents occurred that made the ruling authorities to exile the Bahá'ís and the Azalis to Israel and Cyprus in separate groups. Bahá'u'lláh reached 'Akká (Acre) in present-day Israel together with his family in August 1868 and spent the remainder of his life as a Prisoner living under house arrest at different places. Thus, Israel is regarded as Holy Land for Baha'is besides the other established religions such as Judaism, Christianity and Islam.

In 'Akká, Bahá'u'lláh was imprisoned in a fort for nine years. Later he was allowed to leave the prison to live in a village. He rented a house in a village called Mazriah and began to live there. During the 24 years of his imprisonment and house arrest Baha'u'llah kept himself busy writing or dictating his revelation including his Book of Laws, the Kitáb-i-Aqdas. In this book, he enunciated his vision of a new World Order and the basic principles and aims of the Bahá'í Faith. The Bahá'ís regards this work as their Most Holy Book.

Around 1880, he was granted permission to go Bahji, near 'Akká where twelve years later he died in 1892. During this period he allowed to visit Haifa, a port city about 40 kilometers from 'Akká which today has become the world centre of the Bahá'í Faith. Before his passing, Baha'u'llah, appointed his eldest living son, 'Abdu'l-Bahá (also known as 'Abbás Effendi) (1844-1921) as his successor and authorized interpreter of his teachings. When the young Turks formed the government, he was granted pardon in 1908 and was duly released from prison. After this, he engaged himself completely in spreading the ideas of his mission and travelled to Egypt, Europe and America in the next three years. During the course of his travels, he organized the Baha'i community although it had already been established in North America since1894. In this way he succeeded in spreading his father's Faith far and wide and established scores of communities in Europe and America and also consolidated hundreds of communities in Iran and in the Indian sub-continent.

In 1920, he was honored by the British government with knighthood. The following year, he died and was buried in the same shrine where remains of the Báb have been entombed on Mount Carmel in Haifa.

According to the will of 'Abdu'l-Bahá, his eldest grandson, Shoghi Effendi Rabbáni (1897-1957) was made his successor and he came to be known as the Guardian of the Baha'i Faith. At the time of 'Abdu'l-Bahá passing Shoghi Effendi was studying in Oxford; when the shocking news reached him he was forced to abort his studies and return to Haifa in 1921.

Haifá, as already mentioned had by now become the administrative centre of Bahá'í Faith and over the next 36 years Shoghi Effendi further developed the places associated with the lives of Bahá'u'lláh and 'Abdu'l-Bahá and built the superstructure of the Shrine of the Báb, the International Baha'i Archives and made plans for other important historical structures. In 1937 he married the daughter of a Canadian Baha'i architect, Mary Maxwell. Besides guiding the systematic development of the Bahá'í Community, Shoghi Effendi took great pains to translate some of the most important Writings of Baha'u'llah and 'Abdu'l-Bahá into English. He also wrote extensively and today his collected works number some fifty volumes. Besides the development of the Bahá'í World Centre Shoghi Effendi also inspired the Bahá'í communities to establish Houses of Worship (Bahá'í Temples) and these have become architectural marvels of which the one in New Delhi is the most widely visited.

After Shoghi Effendi died without leaving a will, he had however already prepared the Bahá'í communities around the world through his Ten Year Crusade to elect the supreme legislative body ordained by Bahá'u'lláh in 1963. Accordingly, the Universal House of Justice was elected by secret ballot by members of 57 regional and national Spiritual Assemblies. Since that time the affairs of the Bahá'í communities worldwide have been administered by this international body. It operates from Haifa and is elected every five years through an International Bahá'í Convention at which time national representatives cast their ballots; spend their time in prayers at the Holy Shrines at 'Akká and Haifa besides consulting on the worldwide progress of the Bahá'í community.

Bahá'í religion, emphasizing the establishment of human unity, is an independent and universal religion. Bahá'u'lláh taught religious truth cannot be absolute but progressive and relative to changing times. Thus, the Divine sends his Manifestations to renew the religious teachings from Age to Age—spiritual truths are restated and social teachings are provided according to the needs of the times. Divine revelation may likened to the chapters of the Book of the Knowledge of God. Each time a Manifestation of God appears a new chapter is added. This system of knowledge must complete another system of knowledge called science. The essence of God cannot be incarnated but his attributes and powers can be manifested through a chosen Mouthpiece or Divine Teacher. The Divine Essence is the one that manifests and reveals Itself through the person of perfect human being. That is why this diversity has to be put together as a unity. The foremost duty of the Manifestations of God is to create an all pervading unity in human -kind. Bahá'í Faith is the religion of belief and faith. It is free from man-made interpretations and public religious rituals, worship or customs and conventions. However the following religious duties have been enjoined on the Bahá'ís:

1. Together and observe the 19-Day Feast once every nineteen days, i.e. on the first day of every Bahá'í month (Baha'is have a new calendar).
2. To fast from sunrise to sunset for nineteen days of the last month of the Bahá'í calendar called 'Alá (Loftiness), i.e. 2 – 20 March.
3. To abstain from liquors and other intoxicating products.
4. To pray every day. Prayer is to be offered individually in the privacy of one's home. Public prayer is only allowed for the dead at the time of the funeral ceremony. Prayers can be offered in any language.
5. To promote the core activities namely organizing Devotional Gatherings in Bahá'í homes, participate and facilitate in the conduct of Study Circles, hold Children's Classes, support the Spiritual Empowerment of Junior Youth.

Apart from these duties, several rules and regulations

have been laid down for the organization of a society; for example, 19% of one's annual savings if that reaches a stipulated amount should be offered to the Universal House of Justice as the "Right of God". Every believer must write a Will and make provision for his or her family members as well leave a certain percentage of one's wealth or property for the teacher(s) who were instrumental for his education. In society, men and women are to be treated as possessing equal rights and privileges. Marriage is highly recommended but not obligatory and monogamy is the prescribed norm, the practice of bigamy or polygamy prevalent during the days of Bahá'u'lláh is annulled. For marriage, the consent of the parents of both the bride and the groom is essential. There is a provision for divorce but it is discouraged.

The most significant and original aspects of Bahá'í teaching is the organization of the community according to democratic norms and the pattern of Bahá'í administration it is prophesied would evolve into a new World Order. For the organization of the community first there is a local spiritual assembly, second a national spiritual assembly, and third the Universal House of Justice. In all these assemblies, representatives are elected by secret ballot, and participation in these elections is considered to be a spiritual obligation. The members of the Bahá'í community live in almost three hundred and fifty countries and territories of the world. Their religious literature has been translated into near 800 languages. According to the most recent data obtainable as compiled by Encyclopedia Britannica and the Wikipedia the total number of Bahá'ís worldwide is estimated to be between six to seven million. They are organized into some 185 National Spiritual Assemblies and over 25,000 Local Spiritual Assemblies. In Irán, the birthplace of the Bahá'í Faith, the Baha'is are the largest minority community with a total of over 3.5 lakhs. The Bahá'í religion came to India from the earliest days of its inception with the oldest community being Mumbai (formerly Bombay). There are over one million Baha'is living in different parts of India and some 600 Local Assemblies.

Although Bahá'í religion has no practice of ritual worship, even so the Kitáb-i-Aqdas has permitted the construction of temples called Mashriqu'l-Adhkár (Dawning Place of the Remembrance of God). These are aesthetically built with a dome and nine sides. So far eight such continental House of Worship have been built. These Temples are open to a person of any religion or belief and no one's entry is to be barred. The first such Temple was constructed in Ishqabad which is now in Turkmenistan. It was constructed in 1902 but was destroyed in an earthquake. However, after this in 1912, 'Abdu'l-Bahá himself laid the foundation stone of a Temple for North America at Wilmette in Illinois. Today, Panama, Australia, Germany, Uganda, Samoa and India have similar grand temples. Apart from these, the Bahá'u'lláh's Shrine in Bahji and the Shrines of the Báb and Abdu'l-Bahá in Haifá, are memorable monuments and visited by Bahá'í pilgrims and others in the thousands each year.

(The corrections and inputs by Dr. A. K. Merchant, Trustee, Lotus Temple & National Spiritual Assembly of the Bahá'ís of India)

ZOROASTRIAN

ARTICLE ABOUT ZOROASTRIAN BELIEFS AND HISTORY by Dame Dr. Prof. Meher Master- Moos, President, Zoroastrian College for PROF DR B. B. Puri's New book IN SEARCH OF GOD - ONE SOUL MANY GODS

Historically, ancient Avestan and Sanskrit Vedic are sister languages, originating in the lands of Aryana Vaeja, i.e., former USSR countries mainly of Central Asia. Eg. It is well known that the Sun Deity MITHRA in Avesta became

MITRA in Sanskrit, the plant Haoma in Avesta became Soma in Sanskrit, used in the Avestan Yasna Sanskrit Yagna ceremony; etc.

The extant Avestan texts give the written records of the observations of ancient period Astronomers. Based on the positions of stars contained in the texts of the MITHRA & RASHNA YASHTS (Hymns of praise in honour of these Deities, called Yazatas in Avesta) and the Shatapada Brhamana Sanskrit text, in 1975 the British astronomer Dr John Ponsonby of the Jodrell Bank Observatory in England and late Dr Sohrab Eruch Hakim of Bombay established the date when these Avestan Yashts were written, 9500 years ago; which corroborates the date of holy Paegambar Saheb Asho Spitaman Zarathushtra given by the holy Abed Sahebs of Demavand Kuh to late Ustad Saheb Behramshah Nowroji Shroff. This research also corroborates the work of late Mr. H S Spencer, author of the Aryan Ecliptic Cycle.

Using the computerized SkyGlobe Program the Englishman Adrian Gilbert tracked the exact birth date of Asho Spitaman Zarathushtra as 16th May 7500 BC a few days before the Vernal Equinox occurring in 2 degrees of Cancer; and he also worked out that the other possible date could be the Vernal Equinox in 6594 BC; which corroborates the calculations made astrologically by late Dr Behramshah Pithavala in his book "In Search of Divine Light".

The recorded history of the Pre- Zarathustrian period is found in the extant Avestan books of "Yashts" i.e., Hymns of Praises to the Amesha Spenta and Yazata, (the Deities, of Sanskrit books, the Arch-angels and Angels concepts of Judaism, Christianity and Islam, which were all influenced by the undercurrent golden thread of ancient esoteric wisdom from the Zarathustrian teachings. It is also found in the epic poem Shahnameh of Firdausi, the Khorassani Persian poet and other books. The two main pre-Zarathushtrian dynasties were the Peshdadian and the Kyanian. The recorded names of the Peshdadian monarchs and their main highlights of their reigns are given in these books. Their Persianised names are given here. The original Avestan names are found in the Avestan Yashts. These included the Peshdadian monarchs, Gayomard, Shyamak, Hoshang, Tehmurasp Devbund, Jamshed (who is considered to be the Yima of Sanskrit literature and Noah of the Christian old Bible) who lived for a thousand years and saved all forms of life through the floods after the last Ice Age; Zohak the wicked; Fareidoon, also known as Thraetona, the Healer, and King Minocher.

Then came the Kyanian dynasty, that ruled in Central Asia (the geographical area now known as Tajikistan, Uzbekistan, Afghanistan and surrounding mountain regions) in the country of Bactria with its capital city of Balkh (now in ruins in Afghanistan). Kyanian means Ruler having Kingly Khoreh- ie golden halo light. The monarchs included Kai Kobad, Kai Kaus, Prince Shiavak, Kai Khushroo, Kai Lohrasp, Kai Vishtasp during whose rule Asho Spitama Zarathushtra lived. This last named King became the Patron of Asho Zarathushtra, and he helped to spread the teachings of Zarathushtra in all the neighbouring regions and 5 out of the 21 original books. These include 1. "Visperat", 2. "Vi devo dat"; 3. "Yasna including the Gathas"; 4. "Yashts", and 5. book of daily prayers the "Khordeh Avesta." Out of these, 1, 2 and 3 have come to be used for performance of rituals and ceremonies by the Zoroastrian Priests in India and 4 and 5 are used by all Zoroastrians.

The main Teachings of Asho Spitaman Zarathushtra include the following. Ahura Mazda the Creator of the Universe of Light Energy & Matter, through the power of Sound and Light vibrations created the entire Universe and set it in motion. The Creator is the Purest Holiest White Light of the Universe, in which not a shade or shadow of darkness can be traced. Ahura Mazda had a Plan for the Evolution of Creation. To help him in fulfilling his Divine Plan, he created the Spiritual very very high level Souls of the Amesha Spentas the highest deities- the Archangels. There are 6 Amesha Spentas each having a portfolio in the government of the Universe with specific work allocation. Their Avestan names are Vohu Mano the Good Loving-mind in charge of the animal kingdom on planet Earth ; Asha Vahista, Highest Holiness/Righteousness incharge of the divine Justice and Fire on planet Earth; Khshathra Vairyu the Strength of Ahura Mazda - incharge of the mineral kingdom on planet Earth; Spenta Armaity the Power of White Light incharge of the planet Earth; Hvaretat the Glory of the Halo through which Perfection is attained, incharge of the waters of planet Earth; Ameretat Immortality in charge of the Plants kingdom on planet Earth.

The concept of the Yazata already existed in pre - Zarathushtrian times. These ancient Aryan Deities are listed as 26 in the Yashts; and correspond to the Vedic Deities; eg Avestan Mithra is Vedic Mitra; Avestan Verethregna is Vedic Varuna; Avestan Raam Yazata is Vedic Raam; Avestan Ashishvang is Vedic Laxmi; Avestan Ataar is Vedic Agni; Avestan GoVaat is Vedic Vayu; etc. Asho Zarathushtra arranged them in orderly fashion providing each of the Amesha Spenta the assistance of several Yazatas.

Asho Spitama Zarathushtra's main teaching as a Messenger of Ahura Mazda was that all people, humanity at large should have full knowledge of the Divine Universal Natural Laws of Ahura Mazda. These laws govern all souls in creation. By having this spiritual knowledge the people would voluntarily stop doing anything which was a transgression of the Cosmic laws. Every transgression is a "gunah" *i.e.* violation of Cosmic laws, which has the consequences of making bad darkness in the light of the soul; and thereby preventing the soul in its progress on the Rah E AshA the straight Path of Righteousness/Goodness.

Asho Spitama taught that the best way for anybody to prevent even the faintest shadow from entering the pure white light of the individual person's soul was (and is) to practise in daily life, Good Thoughts Good Words And Good Deeds; and to repent after every few hours of any transgression of any of the Divine laws. By making the light of your own soul Pure & Perfect, then only the soul can progress on the Rah e Asha and become one with, united with, merged in the Purest White Light of the Creator Ahura Mazda. When this happens the soul of the person loses its individuality and becomes totally merged with the Supra Consciousness of the Divine Light of the Creator.

In the words of the English poet Lord Alfred Tennyson this is known as

"That one far off divine event to which the Whole Creation moves."

This practice of Good Thoughts Good Words and Good Deeds which are in obedience of the Divine Cosmic laws, helps to cut the "bad karma" of the individual person; and helps the soul of that individual person to cut free from the cycles of re-birth and re-incarnation under the law of karma, and helps the soul of the individual person to attain Perfection and then Immortality i.e. become one with, (YUGA) joined with, merged in the purest white light of the Creator Ahura Mazda, then the soul is filled with Bliss and Joy. This is the main purpose for which every soul has taken birth on planet earth; and this is the way to achieve the purpose, this Path of Spiritual Salvation. In this manner Asho Spitaman Zarathushtra has shown every person how to cut free from the bondage of the laws of karma and set the soul free to reunite with its Creator. This goal can be achieved in one lifetime, if each soul truly and sincerely leads its life by listening to and obeying its inner Voice of Conscience. Then that person can do no wrong, and can guide others on the Path of Spiritual Salvation.

Thee only do I know to be Supreme. All other I dismiss from this my mind. He who is known as Ahura Mazata with duteous deeps we worship Him alone we know thee as supreme above all lives.

O pilgrims for the shrine! Where go come back! Come back! Ye, where? The beloved is here! His presence in your entire, neighborhood both bless. Why will ye wander in the wilderness!

3(A)

History of Ancient Period

Essence of all religions is humanity which revolves around righteousness, action, creation, sustenance, happiness and ultimate self realization to **who am I and who is HE.**

I like to add that the Vedic culture is ageless, sanatana a religion of wisdom, love and hope for all. It does not divide, but unites, does not injure but heals, does not kill but saves. If you attain God and his kingdom of righteousness, all else shall be added unto you.

One God is the father of all, who is above all, and through all and in you all.

"The wise see in their heart the face of God, and not in the images of stone even clay, who in themselves, as I can see him not. They see to find him in some outer spot."

Religions promise you to show the path to enlightenment which is a blissful state of consciousness.

Whatever small knowledge I possess from all religions I founded a Research institute of Vedic Culture NGO, where we do research in Vedic philosophy and teach the spiritual vows of vedic philosophy on this subject. I have got the opportunity to write number of books on vedic philosophy, such as **A practical guide to an Ageless Mind, The Art of**

blissful living, Vastu Science 21st century to enjoy the gift of nature, and Life before Death, which I recommend to my readers to read these books of knowledge and learn the spiritual laws of vedic philosophy.

To Conclude

Religion everywhere has served the purpose of supporting the moral & social principles which have made men civilized.

To all religions - My salutation again and again to all, also my salutation to the truth of all religions.

The source of creation from the nature, by the nature or God is functioning within, or from your five senses you can feel that the God is within you. The question is whether you can see the God or not. The spiritual person can feel within himself and within every moment when we say God, or soul we are talking about the basis of physical creation. This dimension cannot be perceived through our five senses.

Yes, we can achieve through our karma. Karma is of many kinds, different layers and dimensions.

MOTHER OF UNIVERSE Durga Maa adi shakti

LORD SHIVA

LORD RAMA

LORD KRISHNA
PERIOD OF BHAGAVAD - GITA

ANCIENT PERIOD

PERIOD Of RIG VEDA
1500- 1000 BC

HISTORICAL VEDIC RELIGION EVOLVES INTO EARLY CLASSICAL HINDUISM
600 BC

AGE OF BUDDHA
566-486 BC

AGE OF MAHAVIRA
540-467 BC

BIRTH OF JESUS CHRIST
BC 0 AD

BIRTH OF PROPHET MUHAMMAD
570 AD

ADI SHANKARCHARYA PREACHES HIS PHILOSOPHY
600 AD

RAMANUJA PREACHES HIS VAISHNAVA PHILOSOPHY
1050 AD

GURU NANAK, The Founder Of Sikhism Was Born
1469 AD

AGE OF SAINT-POET KAVIRA AND THE BHAKTI MOVEMENT
1450 -1518 AD

AGE OF MAHAPRABHU CHAITANYA AND VAISHNAV MOVEMENT
1486 - 1534 AD

LIFETIME OF GREAT DEVOTEE TULSIDAS
1532 - 1623 AD

BRAHMO SAMAJ STARTED MOVEMENT UNDER RAJA RAMMOHAN ROY
1772-1833 AD

DAYANANDA SARASWATI FOUNDED ARYA SAMAJ
1824 -1883 AD

SRI RAMAKRISHNA TEACHED JATA MAT TATA PATH
1836 - 1886 AD

SWAMI VIVEKANANDA
1863 - 1902 AD

SRI AUROBINDO PREARCHED HIS PHILOSOPHY OF HUMAN PROGRESS AND SPIRITUAL EVOLUTION
1872 - 1950 AD

3(B)

Modern Heroes of 21st Century who changed the world

MOHANDAS KARAMCHAND GANDHI, POLITICAL LEADER

About Him :

While it may come as a surprise to many, Gandhi (as he is called) was neither the father of Indian nationalism nor particularly politically influential in the early days of the independence movement. On the contrary: well educated and a lawyer, he was English oriented but Indian by heart. He spent time in England, a country that he considered to be the center of modern civilization at that time. More, as he experimented with English ways, he also became a citizen of the world.

In fact, the great Gandhi was not radicalized until he moved to South Africa and tried to practice law amid the extremes of apartheid and white supremacy: Once he returned to India, he became an advocate of non-violence and non-cooperation, and almost immediately had the opportunity to implement those ideals when he began to play center stage in the political and economic life of India and the Raj. In his autobiography, *The Story of My Experiments with Truth, (50 plus one Great Books You Should Have Read, Encouragement Press, 2006)* he clearly states his position on nonviolence: "There are many causes I am prepared to die for but no causes I am prepared to kill for."

MOTHER TERESA, SOCIAL REFORMER

About Her :

Mother Teresa is surely one of the most famous names of the last 50 years, having garnered almost every honor and award for her tireless work with the homeless and poor in India.

The confidante of popes and presidents, she was awarded a state funeral in India upon her death. But it is her life, not her death, that continues to motivate and inspire men and women of goodwill to care for the homeless, children with HIV and victims everywhere.

BILL GATES, BUSINESSMAN

About Him :

What is it like to be the richest man in the world, a man whose wealth at one point exceeded $100 billion, according to Forbes magazine? And what is it like to give a huge portion of this wealth to charities and good works the world over? Bill Gates, perhaps the capitalist's capitalist, founded a company that revolutionized every aspect of business, education, communication and entertainment, yet maintains a relatively low profile considering his personal and business success.

However whether, he is viewed, admired or not he is still a hero to millions, because he made information and technology available for a relatively low price. He is the master of business acumen, inspiring tens of thousands to form their own companies and to attempt to take technology and computing to new levels of sophistication and service.

MARTIN LUTHER KING JR., PROMINENT LEADER IN THE AFRICAN-AMERICAN CIVIL RIGHTS MOVEMENT

About Him :

Entire generations have seen, and future generations will continue to see, the famous speech delivered in Washington during the height of the civil rights movement, *I Have a Dream*. Here stands the inspiring image of a man who had devoted his entire life to improving the rights of African Americans, not only in the South but also the segregated cities of the North.

How, he asked, could an entire segment of the United States be relegated to second or third class status ? How was it possible, 100 years after the Civil War, that blacks had less freedom and equality? Well, it was his mission to do something about it, regardless of the cost or sacrifices.

NEIL ALDEN ARMSTRONG, ASTRONAUT

About Him :

Heroes are often the stuff of firsts to navigate around the world, to fly across the Atlantic, to climb Mt. Everest and dozens more. Certainly any individual with the courage to land on the moon with what could be described, at best, as very tentative technology and planning, has to be one of our heroes.

The wonder of Neil Armstrong is the complete lack of ego and ambition beyond his desire to be part of the NASA mission and program. Whether active or retired, he accepted the admiration of millions with the humility of a child. His right kind of stuff can hardly be underestimated, and his superior intellectual ability helped NASA with an ambitious and politically sensitive mission to the moon.

NELSON ROLIHLAHLA MANDELA,
CIVIL RIGHTS LEADER

About Him :

Imagine spending 27 years of your life in prison, most

of them in one of the most brutal and horrible places in South Africa. People have survived and will continue to survive long years of confinement, but to do so with your values, dignity and principles intact is another story.

While he is lauded by most of the people of world, it is important to note that Mandela once advocated violence. Whether terrorist or hero, there can be no doubt that Mandela emerged as a nation builder- a nation of blacks and whites.

A matter of great significance, often overlooked during Mandela's amazing career, is that he ensured a transition from a white dominated society to an all inclusive government without further violence or upheaval.

The Legacy of the Mandela

Mandela will always be a symbol of courage and forbearance under difficult conditions. He saw an unfair system and tried to help stop it in the face of incredible odds. He was able to use his intelligence and education to articulate strong positions, make logical arguments against the very nature of apartheid and attract the loyalty and devotion of not only a small number of supporters in the ANC, but in his country and the entire world.

It is almost impossible to imagine staying imprisoned for almost three decades and still being able to inspire followers into staying the course. However, this is what Mandela did, and his ultimate reward was his release (untainted by charges that he compromised his principles just to get out of prison) and the presidency of the country. It was an amazing change of fortune.

Mandela's main legacy as president of South Africa is the progress that was made in peaceful relations between the blacks and the Afrikaner-dominated apartheid parties. Instead of calling for reprisals against the white minority, he worked hard with former President F.W. de Klerk to bring the two races together for the common good.

After Mandela's retirement, he was showered with accolades and awards, the highlight being the Nobel Peace Prize in 1993. Other honours he received included the order of Merit and order of St. John from British Queen Elizabeth II, the Presidential Medal of Freedom from President George W. Bush and honorary citizenship from Canada (the only living foreigner to be given this).

Mandela has emerged as a hero, but no hero is perfect. By any standard, however, he showed the courage and perseverance to inspire his people and change his nation forever.

ANNA HAZARE, LEADER 2011

About Him :

He once contemplated suicide and even wrote a two-page essay also on why he wanted to end his life. Anna Hazare was not driven to such a pass by circumstances, he wanted to live no more, because he was frustrated with life and wanted an answer to the purpose of human existence.

The story goes like that, one day, at the New Delhi Railway Station, he chanced upon a book on Swami Vivekananda. Drawn by Vivekananda's photograph, he was quoted as saying that he read the book and found his answer-that the motive of his life lay in service to his fellow humans.

For Anna Hazare, it was another battle, and he has fought quite a few, including some as a soldier for 15 years in Indian Army and enlisted himself after the 1962 Indo-China war when the government exhorted young men to join the Army.

In 1978, he took voluntary retirement from the 9th Maratha Battalion and returned home to Ralegaon Siddhi, a village in Maharashtra's drought-prone Ahmadnagar. He was 39 years old at that time.

He found farmers back home struggling for survival and their suffering would prompt him to pioneer rainwater conservation that put his little hamlet on the international map as a model village.

The villagers revered him. Thakaram Raut, a school teacher in Ralegaon Siddhi says, "Thanks to Anna's agitations, we got a school, we got electricity, we got development schemes for farmers."

Anna Hazare's fight against corruption began. He fought first against corruption that was blocking growth in rural India. His organization is the Bhrashtachar Virodhi Jan Andolan (People's movement against Corruption), his tool of protest is hunger strikes, and his prime target are politicians.

The Gandhian is soldiering on from one battle to another in his war against corruption. He fought from the front to have Right to Information (RTI) implemented. He is now fighting for the implementation of the Jan Lokpal Bill, the anti-corruption bill drafted by his team of crusaders.

August 2011, Anna Hazare is the face of India's fight against corruption. He has taken that fight to the corridors of power and challenged the government at the highest level. People, the common man and well-known personalities alike, have supported him in the hundreds swelling to the thousands.

4

Religion starts where science ends. The begining of higher wisdom

(As I learn from Bhagavad Gita)

God is the focal point of religion. Faith in God inspires a principled life. Thus religion has a close relationship with God and principled conduct. In almost all religions and ethical books, the supremacy of God has been accepted.

God is fundamental to religion. Faith in God and religion generates energy in man. Man is not completely capable and he often finds himself incomplete and helpless. Social, economic and political principles and ideals cannot liberate him from this state. Man renews his energy by faith in God and in his religion.

Unity in society can only be established by considering God as One. Political principles and economic systems create differences, make man's point of view narrow, whereas faith in God and trust in religion brings about harmony between an individual and society. Faith in God makes our tendencies pure, our point of view generous and conduct benevolent. It develops feelings of friendship, sacrifice, tolerance, love and affection.

To lead a happy, prosperous life free of worries, it is necessary to have unshakeable faith in God and trust in ethical conduct and behavior. Plato has also said in his well-known book "Republic" that until a nation believes in God, it cannot become strong. This same faith in God has brought man from the primitive state to the modern space age.

Faith in God has filled man with the feeling of good for all. This faith has played a significant role in the rise of religion and its development.

Not only this, faith in God has enriched literature, music and the various arts; it drew man towards contemplation and consequently religious literature and philosophy were born. The study of religious philosophy helps in establishing harmony between various religions.

All religions expound one truth. The goal of all is one. Differences are only visible in the means and in the modes of rituals. But this also is only superficial. In their fundamental form, there is a similarity. Today, man has become more intellectual. He wants every curiosity, every doubt to be resolved on a mental plane. He needs an intellectual and scientific analysis of everything. Religious philosophy attempts to make religion intellectual and scientific.

If we read and try to understand the other religions, it would become clear that the fundamental elements in all religions are basically the same.

The differences of opinion that have arisen with regard to the form of God are the result of the influences of particular times and traditions. But the fundamental is the same in all.

Almost all religions of the world have their origin in Asia and their study shows that not only in the fundamentals but also in their outward form there is basic similarity.

Mahatma Gandhi's favourite line Ishwar and Allah are both your names, is not merely an emotional response. A deep and eternal meaning is hidden in these words.

In the Gita, Krishna tells Arjuna 'I am the light of the moon and the sun'.

In the Holy Koran, it has been said,' Allah is the light of the skies and the earth.' the Gita calls God the 'Lord of all'.

Sanskrit Shloka:-

bhumir apo' nalo vayuh kham man buddhir eva ca
ahankara itiyam me bhinna prakrtir astadha

Bhagavad-gita 7.4

This means: -Earth, water, fire, air, ether, mind, intelligence and false ego all together these eight constitute. My separated material energies.

The science of God analyzes the constitutional position of God and His diverse energies. Material nature is called prakarti, or the energy of the Lord in his different purusa incarnations.

"For material creation, Lord Krishna's plenary expansion assumes three Vishnus. The first one, Maha-Vishnu, creates the total material energy, known as the mahat-tattva. The second, Garbhodakasayi Vishnu, enters into all the universes to create diversities in each of them. The third, Ksirodakasayi Vishnu, is diffused as the all pervading Supersoul in all the universes and is known as paramatma. He is present even within the atoms. Anyone who knows these three Vishnus can be liberated from material entanglement.

This material world is a temporary manifestation of one of the energies of the Lord. All the activities of the material world are directed by these three Vishnu expansions of Lord Krishna. These purusas are called incarnations.

Generally one who does not know the science of God (Krishna) assumes that this material world is for the enjoyment of the living entities and that the living entities are the purusas the causes, controllers and enjoyers of the material energy.

In the verse under discussion it is stated that Krishna is the original cause of the material manifestation. The ingredients of the material manifestation are separated energies of the Lord, which is the ultimate goal of the impersonalists, is a spiritual energy manifested in the spiritual sky.

In the material energy, the principal manifestations are eight, as above mentioned. Out of these, the first five manifestations, namely earth, water, fire, air and sky, are called the five gigantic creations or the gross creations, within which the sense objects are included.

They are the manifestations of physical sound, touch, form, taste and smell.

Material science comprises these ten items and nothing more. But the other three items, namely mind, intelligence and false ego, are neglected by the materialists. Philosophers who deal with mental activities are also not perfect in knowledge because they do not know the ultimate source. The false ego "I am," and "It is mine," which constitute the basic principle of material existence.

In the Koran Majid, God has been called the 'Lord of the entire world'.

Sanskrit Saloka:

raso 'ham apsu kaunteya prabhasmi sai- suryayoh
pranavah sarva-vedesu sabdah khe paurusam nrsu

Bhagavad-gita 7.8

This means: - O son of Kunti, I am the taste of water, the light of the sun and the moon, the syllable om in the Vedic mantras; I am the sound in ether and ability in man.

The codes created by God also have a similarity. According to the Bible, "Every pure treatise has been created through the inspiration of God and is useful for preaching, for teaching, for self-improvement and religious instruction".

Their meaning and goals are one. Their teachings are the same wisdom, the same which has been given to humanity through their means. If there is difference, it is in their descriptions, which have adopted different modes, keeping in mind different listeners".

Sanskrit Shloka:-

Imam vivasvate yogam proktavan aham avyayam
vivasvan manave praha manur iksvakave bravit

***Bhagavad-gita* 4.1**

This means: - The personality of Godhead, Lord Sri Krishna, said: I instructed this imperishable science of yoga to the Sun-God, Vivasvan, and Vivasvan instructed it to Manu, the father of mankind, and Manu in turn instructed it to Iksvaku.

Herein we find the history of the Bhagavad-gita traced from a remote time when it was delivered to the royal order of all planets, beginning from the sun planet. The kings of all planets are especially meant for the protection of the inhabitants, and therefore the royal order should understand the science of Bhagavad Gita in order to be able to rule the citizens and protect them from material bondage to lust. Human life is meant for cultivation of spiritual knowledge, in eternal relationship with the Supreme Personality of Godhead, and the executive heads of all states and all planets are obliged to impart this lesson to the citizens by education, culture and devotion. In other words, the executive heads of all states are intended to spread the science of Krishna consciousness so that the people may take advantage of this great science and pursue a successful path, utilizing the opportunity of the human form of life.

In this millennium, the sun-god is known as Vivasvan, the king of the sun, which is the origin of all planets within the solar system.

This knowledge, gained through tradition, came to be known by the royal sages.

Sanskrit Shloka:-

evam parampara-praptam imam rajarsayo viduh
sa kaleneha mahata yogo nastah parantapa

***Bhagavad-gita* 4.2**

> **This means:** - this supreme science was thus received through the chain of disciplic succession, and the saintly kings understood it in that way. But in course of time the succession was broken, and therefore the science as it is appears to be lost.

It is clearly stated that the Gita was especially meant for the saintly kings because they were to execute its purpose in ruling over the citizens. Certainly Bhagavad-gita was never meant for the demonic persons, who would dissipate its value for no one's benefit and would devise all types of interpretations according to personal whims. As soon as the original purpose was scattered by the motives of the unscrupulous commentators, there arose the need to re-establish the disciplic succession. Five thousand years ago it was detected by the Lord Himself that the purpose of the Gita appeared to be lost. In the same way, at the present moment also, there are innumerable interpretations rendered by different mundane scholars, but almost all of them do not accept the supreme Personality of Godhead, Krishna, although they make a good business on the words of Sri Krishna. This spirit is demonic, because demons do not believe in God but simply enjoy the property of the Supreme. Since there is a great need of an edition of the Gita in English, as it is received by the parampard (disciplic succession) system, an attempt is made herewith to fulfill this great want. Bhagavad-gita accepted as it is a great boon to humanity; but if it is accepted as a treatise of philosophical speculations, it is simply a waste of time.

No instance of conversion to Hinduism and Buddhism gh force or inducement is found in history.

Many Brahmin scholars have not only initiated hism voluntarily but have also further strengthened its sophical base.

eligious teachers are true followers of religion and it is grave responsibility that, through mutual dialogue, they ish the truth declared in all religions that God is one.

rit Shloka:-

cetasa sarva-karmani mayi sannyasya mat-parah
buddhi-yogam upasritya mac-cittah satatam bhava

Bhagavad-gita18.57

his means: - In all activities just depend upon e and work always under My protection. In such evotional service, be fully conscious of Me.

it Shloka:-

mac-cittah sarva-durgani mat-prasadat tarisyasi
atha cet tvam ahankaran na srosyasi vinanksyasi

Bhagavad-gita 18.58

is means: - if you become conscious of me, you ll pass over all the obstacles of conditioned life my grace. If, however, you do not work in such nsciousness but act through false ego, not ring me, you will be lost.

t Shloka:-

isavrah sava-butanam hrd-dese rjuna tisthati
bhramayan sarva-bhtani yantrarudhani mayaya

Bhagavad-gita 18.61

s means: - the supreme lord is situated in ryone's heart as supersoul, O Arjuna, and is cting the wanderings of all living entities, who

Similarly, in different religions and their treatises, we find several teachings which inspire man to follow good conduct and see God in every one.

Sanskrit Shloka:-

Sarva-bhuta-stham atmanam sarva-bhutani catmani
iksate yoga-yuktatma sarvatra sama-darsanah

Bhagavad-gita 6.29

This means : - A true yogi observes Me in all beings and also sees every being in Me. Indeed, the self-realized person sees Me, the same supreme Lord, everywhere.

This is the basic mantra for the feeling of universal brotherhood and the desire for the well-being of all. All religions teach ethical conduct. Hindu treaties also do the same. Their impact has been profound on Solomon, Jesus Christ and Prophet Mohammad. The compassion and non-violence of Lord Buddha is well known throughout the world.

Prayer and worship have been made an essential part of the day in every religion. Vedic prayer and worship, the Buddhist prayer, the Christian prayer, the Namaz of Islam, all have the same goal. According to one scholar, the word Namaz comes from the root word Nam of Nayan in Sanskrit, together with Aj, that is God. Bowing in front of God, that is, Namaz.

The concept of places of pilgrimage is also similar everywhere. The Char Dham of Hindus and other such places are well-known. It is said that before his great salvation, Lord Buddha advised his disciples to accept Lumbini (his birth place), Bodh Gaya (the place of enlightenment), and Sarnath (the place of the first sermon) as pilgrimage places. Kushinagar (the Place of his great nirvana) was also added to this list later.

Apart from Kaba, Mecca and Madina, other holy places of the Muslims include Najaj and Karbala.

Christians also consider the pilgrimage to places connected with the birth of Christ and his works, as blessed.

In all religions, the fundamental truth and the basic teachings are almost the same. Their chief aim is to obtain God.

(Patience, self-control, forgiveness, truth are among the ten characteristics of Dharma)

In the Bible it has been said:

- You will not kill.
- You will not give false evidence.
- You will not steal.
- You will not commit adultery
- You will not covet your neighbour's goods.

The Holy Koran also warns against killing, lying, stealing and adultery.

We are directed to respect our mother, father and elders of all religions. But this is the irony of mankind that it's different societies, (in spite of believing in God and being religious), have made non-controversial issues controversial and continued to shed blood. God and religion teach us mercy, compassion and love. But even those who accept these teachings do just the opposite.

Our paths may be different, but our goal is one. It is ironical that our religions give rise to so many sects in the course of time and such great differences get embedded in them that their followers become thirsty for each other's blood. Several instances of this nature can be found in history.

History is full of instances of terrifying bloodshed engineered by religious frenzy and instances of forcible conversions. Such forcible conversions nurture mutual hatred even after centuries. It is unfortunate that we do not learn anything from history.

If God is One and all religions have unshakeable faith in Him, then why is there bloodshed in the name of God or

religion? Why we are fighting with ea
agitates not only intellectuals but ordi

But it would be wrong to blame G
bloodshed and struggles. We are at faul
violence born of religious frenzy. We
the books of the major religions and w
advocacy for violence, animosity and h
taught us to love and to see everyone

All religions are over 2000 years
in their thought and beliefs. All relig
all religions have the same goal. The t
are for the good of mankind. Then
the attempts at conversion? Why t
religion as inferior to another? Hen
day that the teachers and heads of
and evolve a code by which followe
the religion of others and desist fron
on others.

It is necessary to do this to m
and useful for people. Otherwise
name of religions will create dou
and meaning among the minds of i
without religion will be even mor

Today, when the world i
dismantling of geographical boun
to caution ordinary people about t
into religious boundaries and cre
their own self-interest. People
instrument of fulfilling their ow
found in every religion. In such
religions, after mutual dialogu
feeling of equality among them all
organization to propagate the a
separate and control those who
fulfilling their vested interests.

throu

Budd
philo

their
estab

Sansk

T
M
d

Sansk

Th
wi
by
co
he

Sanskr

Th
eve
dir

are seated as on a machine, made of the material energy.

Arjuna was not the supreme knower, and his decision to fight or not to fight was confined to his limited discretion. Lord Krishna instructed that the individual is not all in all. The supreme personality of Godhead, or He Himself, Krishna, as the localized supersoul, sits in the heart directing the living being. After changing bodies, the living entity forgets his past deeds, but the supersoul, as the knower of the past, present and future, remains the witness of all his activities. Therefore all the activities of living entities are directed by this supersoul. The living entity gets what he deserves and is carried by the material body, which is created in the material energy under the direction of the supersoul. As soon as a living entity is placed in a particular type of body, he has to work under the spell of that bodily situation.

A person seated in a high-speed motorcar drives faster than one seated in a slower moving car, though the living entities, the drivers, may be the same, similarly, by the order of the supreme soul, material nature fashions a particular type of body to a particular type of living entity so that he may work according to his past desires. The living entity is not independent. One should not think himself independent of the supreme personality of Godhead. The individual is always under the Lord's control. Therefore one's duty is to surrender, to him.

Sanskrit Shloka:-

tam eva saranam gaccha sarva-bhavena bharata
tat-prasadat param santim sthanam prapsyasi sasvatam

Bhagavad-gita 18.62

This means: - O scion of Bharata, surrender unto him utterly. By his grace you will attain transcendental peace and the supreme and eternal abode.

A living entity should therefore surrender unto the supreme personality of Godhead, who is situated in everyone's heart, and that will relieve him from all kinds of miseries of this material existence. By such surrender, not only will one be released from all miseries in this life, but at the end he will reach the supreme God.

The "soul" is defined as a non-material, eternal spiritual entity present within any living being. The symptom of the presence of the soul within a body is consciousness. The soul continues to exist after the destruction of the body and it existed prior to the creation of the body. The material body develops, changes and produces by-products [offspring] because of the presence of the soul within. The material body deteriorates in due cause of time and when it is no longer a suitable residence for the soul, it is forced to leave the body. This we call death.

Sanskrit Shloka:-

Tamas tv ajnana-jam viddhi
mohanam sarva-dehinam
Pramadalasys-nidrabhis
Tan nibadhati bharata

Bhagavad Gita 14.8

This means: - O son of Bharata, know that the mode of darkness, born of ignorance, is the delusion of all embodies living entities. The results of this mode are madness, indolence and sleep, which bind the conditioned soul.

In this verse the specific application of the word *Tamas tu* is very significant. This means that the mode of ignorance is a very peculiar qualification of the embodied soul. The mode of ignorance is just the opposite of the mode of goodness. In the mode of goodness, by development of knowledge, one can understand what is what, but the mode of ignorance is just the opposite. Everyone under the spell of the mode of ignorance becomes mad, and a madman cannot understand what is what. Instead of making advancement, one becomes degraded. The definitions of the mode of ignorance is stated in the Vedic literature.

The "Soul Theory" stands completely on its own. It says nothing about the existence or non-existence of God. Although most religious people accept the concept of something other than matter that continues to exist after death and carries the person on to another life there are also atheists who accept such an entity exists. In Hindustan there are both theistic and atheistic philosophies accepting the presence of the soul. It is a compelling and convincing explanation of many things we experience.

The gross material energy consists of earth, water, fire, air and ether [defined as the "space" within the universe]. The subtle material energy consists of mind, intelligence and false-ego [defined as the identification of the body as the self]. The spiritual energy consists of the soul [the individual living entities] and the super-soul. The presence of the soul in any living entity is indicated by consciousness. Although we cannot actually see the soul, we can see its symptoms. We cannot "see" electricity but when we see an illuminated light-globe we can see the symptom of the presence of electricity. Similarly when we see consciousness we see the symptom of the soul.

Any material body inhabited by a soul will undergo changes. It will be created, it will grow, it will produce by-products [offspring], it will dwindle and ultimately it will die.

A spiritual particle present within any living entity whose presence causes the entire body to be pervaded by consciousness is the symptom of the soul. The soul is eternal, it has no birth and it never dies. The soul is the "person within the body", or "the ghost in the machine". At the time of "death" the soul leaves the body and is transferred to the womb of it's next mother's womb according to it's accumulated "karma".

Any material body inhabited by a soul will undergo changes. It will be created, it will grow; it will produce by-products [offspring], it will dwindle and ultimately it will die.

Karma

Karma means literally "actions". It is described by the physical law that each action has an equal and opposite reaction. This universal law is not limited to physical actions, it works for any action. If we commit violence against another, the reactions are generated and we must experience violence upon ourselves in the future. This "karma" or the reactions to our actions is not immediate. The karma is stored in our hearts and it will mature and fructify in due course. If at the time of death there are still karmic reactions stored within the heart which we have not yet experienced then we have to take birth again in the material world in a body suitable to enjoy and suffer the stored karma.

Sanskrit Shloka:-

Sa evayam may ate' dya Yogah proktah puratanah
bhakto' si me sakha ceti rahasyam hy etad uttamam

This means : - That very ancient science of the relationship with the supreme is today told by Me to you because you are My devotee as well as My friend and can therefore understand the transcendental mystery of this science.

There are two classes of men, namely the devotee and the demon. The lord selected Arjuna as the recipient of this great science owing to his being a devotee of the lord, but for the demon it is not possible to understand this great mysterious science. There are a number of editions Gita, the great book of knowledge. Some of them have commentaries by the devotees, and some of them have commentaries by the demons. Commentation by the devotees is real, whereas that of the demons is useless. Arjuna accepts Sri Krishna as the supreme personality of Godhead, and commentary on the Gita following in the footsteps of Arjuna is real devotional service to the cause of this great science. The demonic, however, do not accept lord Krishna as He is. Instead they concoct something about Krishna and mislead general readers from the path of Krishna's instructions. Here is a warning about such misleading paths. One should try to follow the disciplic succession from Arjuna, and thus be benefited by this great science of Srimad Bhagavad-Gita.

Sanskrit shloka:-

Brahmany adhaya karmani
sangam tyaktva karoti yah
Lipyate na sa papena
padma-patram ivambhasa

Bhagavad-gita 5.10

This means : - One who performs his duty without attachment, surrendering the results unto the supreme Lord, is unaffected by sinful action, as the lotus leaf is untouched by water.

5

Philosophy of Rebirth and Reincarnation

Rebirth is the philosophy of the Hindu religion. All other religions advocate the same philosophy?

Sikhism, Jainism and Buddhism also adhere to the philosophy of rebirth.

What is the meaning of rebirth. What relevance does it have to the common man?

The literal meaning of rebirth is the act of the soul casting off the body in which it had lived and inhabiting a new body, one which will be conducive to its evolution.

This is incredibly significant for people, for the undeniable implication is that our "lives" are not merely limited we spend in this current body, but rather we will live again and again. Intricately connected to the philosophy of rebirth is the philosophy of Karma, for it is our karma which determines the body that our soul will inhabit next. Our karma determines both the positive and the negative situations in which our soul will find itself in future. Thus, if we cause pain to others in this life, it is likely that we will experience pain, both in this birth and in the future.

Relevance of Rebirth

The belief in this philosophy serves several purposes for people. First, it ensures that we live our lives honestly, compassionately and purely. If we fully understand that our present actions determine our future circumstances, then we will act with discretion, love, peace and generosity. When we realize that every action is being recorded.

However, the belief in this philosophy also provides hope to people. We see that this life is not our only chance. If someone has lived a life of greed, of lust, of anger and of adharma and if he does believe in this philosophy of rebirth, then he would feel hopeless and fated to an eternity of "Hell." on the other hand, rebirth offers him another chance. The laws of rebirth and karma say, "Your future begins right now. Change yourself today so that your future may be bright."

What is the reasoning and purpose behind rebirth?

There are several purposes to rebirth. The first purpose lies in the realization that as humans we are weak. We succumb to temptation, to desire and to our emotions. Rebirth offers us a vision of life as a continuation from low to high, from impure to pure, and from human to divine. The law of rebirth allows us to both accept our "humanness" graciously without feeling damned to a life in Hell, while simultaneously striving to live our lives in a way that will ensure a positive tomorrow.

How many times can a soul take birth. Can a soul say that's enough, now I do not want to be reborn. Is this request ever accepted?

A soul will come to Earth in human form as many times as are necessary to attain the final state of liberation. The faster one progresses, the fewer births that are necessary. Yes, a soul can certainly decide that this is enough and that it does not want to be reborn. However, simply wanting liberation is not enough. One must work for it. This is the point of sadhana, of seva, of japa, of meditation, of yoga. Through these ways, the soul sheds layer after layer of illusion, ignorance, attachment and desire. Once the layers have all been shed, once the soul realizes its true, divine nature, then rebirth is not necessary. Through these disciplines one can break the cycle of birth and death.

In the Bhagavad Gita, Bhagwan Krishna says:

Sanskrit Shloka:-

Yat karosi yad asnasi, yaj juhosi dadasi yat
Yat tapasyasi kaunteya, tat kurusva mad-arpanam.
Subhasubha-phalair evam moksyase karmabandhanih
Sannyasa-yoga- yuktatma vimukto mam upaisyasi

This means : - "Whatever you do, whatever you eat, whatever you give, and whatever sadhana and tapasya you perform, do everything as an offering to me. In this way you will be freed from the bondage of karma and from the results of karma in your life. Through this renunciation of everything unto me, you will be free of all bondage and you will become united with me."

Can a person really have any knowledge of a previous birth? If so is this knowledge beneficial or does it have disadvantages?

Usually people cannot remember previous births. One must perform great sadhana or go to the saints or special jyotishi (expert astrologer) to learn about their previous births. It is usually not advantageous to know, which is why the Divine Plan does not give us easy access to that information. We have enough trouble trying to navigate through one life, with one husband or wife, one mother, one father, one job, etc. Imagine if we immediately recognized others as our previous parents or spouses or vicious enemies? It would be impossible to remain neutral and unbiased.

Imagine that a man is married to a woman with whom he is not deeply in love. Certainly he loves her but not passionately or deeply. However, due to his duties, he stays married and lives an upright life. Now, imagine that one day he sees a very old woman in the grocery store and immediately recognizes her as his beloved from an earlier birth, he would have great difficulty not leaving his wife and family for an old woman whom he lusted so passionately in an earlier life!

So, in this way our lives would be quite difficult if we remembered our earlier births. Additionally, people talk about remembering our "last life," but how many lives do we want to remember? One, three, ten, fifty? Where would we stop? Eventually, we would be living in a situation where many people we met had played some role in an earlier birth, thus preventing us from treating them fairly and dispassionately in this birth.

Why should the soul take birth on earth only? After leaving the human body, can a soul be born in any other form?

When we realize the purpose of rebirth, then it becomes clear as to why the Earth is the best-suited place and why the human body is the best-suited medium. The purpose, as we have discussed, is to work through previous karmas, to become desireless (through either fulfillment of the desires or through sadhana to eradicate the desires), and to attain God's realization. The human body with its intellect, compassion, consciousness, yearning, understanding and wisdom is most conducive to attain God's realization. As an animal, our lives would be spent solely in eating, sleeping, protecting ourselves and reproducing. There is no time or ability for sadhana. Similarly for plants and other species the consciousness is there in terms of ability to feel pain and to reproduce, but there is not a well developed enough sense to search for something higher.

However, occasionally, due to the performance of truly evil deeds and the accumulation of significant negative karma, a soul will have to come to earth in the form of an insect or lower life form. However, as soon as the lessons are learned in that life form, then again the soul can come in the form of a human, in order to continue its progression toward God's realization.

How many times does a soul have to take birth? Does the same soul always take birth on earth? When he is born, does he look the same each time?

First of all, the soul never actually takes birth. Rather, the soul inhabits human bodies in order to come to Earth, the Karma Bhoomi (land of karma) so that it can engage itself in actions which will lead to its liberation. The individual soul which is intricately connected to the mind, the senses and the desires come to the Earth in those situations which will be most conducive to working through past karmas, to enabling the mind to become pure and desireless, and to helping it attain salvation.

If we have good parents, brothers, sisters, friends and gurus, how can we have the same relatives and friends in the next life? Does a soul have any right to select his family and friends?

There are two important points. Yes, on the one hand we can hope to be with certain people again in our next life. The only way to do this is through prayer. It is not a matter of the soul having a "right" to choose. But, rather, if someone prays with great sincerity, purity and devotion, God can answer the prayer.

However, the other important point is that the purpose of life is NOT to become so attached to our family and friends that we are already worried about not being with them in our next birth. We have a hard enough time living together in this life! So many times we cannot even get along with our family members in this life; we must focus on loving and caring for each other now, rather than be concerned about whether we will be together in the future.

Also, when a soul departs from the body, the soul continues its journey towards God's realization. The scriptures caution us against thwarting the progress of other souls. By begging to stay together with someone, we are inhibiting their own progress and path.

Thus, let us instead concentrate on loving those we are with us now. Let us care for all those who come into our path. Let us pray to move forward with each birth, and let us not be so attached that we sacrifice our own or someone else's spiritual growth in order to simply stay together.

Does the karma of this life become useful in the next life? If the present life is happy, does that mean the soul has done good deeds? On the contrary, if this life is full of unhappiness, does that mean the soul is suffering from his own misdeeds of his last birth?

Yes, the karma of this life is extremely relevant to our next life. However, the equation is not as simple as just good deeds in one life lead to happiness in the next, or bad deeds lead to unhappiness. First of all, karma can take place immediately; it does not necessarily wait until the next birth. We always reap that which we sow. therefore, performing good deeds with a selfless motive will definitely lead to positive karma, both in this life and in future lives.

God has given us a great gift of life. Through this life we have the opportunity to move closer to Him and closer to the heavenly Abode. However, if we throw away this opportunity, then we lose the chance. People, especially youth, make the tragic mistake of thinking that suicide will give them a "fresh start" on a new life. But it is exactly the opposite. By committing suicide they condemn themselves to lifetimes of not only the exact problems they faced in this life, but also to the negative karma accrued by killing themselves. Thus, their next

life will inevitably be much more problematic and much more painful than this one.

Some people donate arms, eyes, and kidneys after death. Some cultures give their bodies to vultures. Do these good deeds at the end of life help the soul for rebirth. Are they beneficial to the soul or does the soul have to suffer for the broken body?

Whatever we do, in life or death, that helps others is a good deed. We should help others as much as we can during life, and if in death we can help them further, then we should do that as well. There is a tradition when saints die they are not cremated, but rather their bodies are floated down Ganga. The reason for this is so that the fish and other animals can gain nourishment from their bodies. The lives of saints are lived for humanity, and even in death they want every cell to be useful to another creature.

So, the soul certainly does not have to suffer through donating organs, and in fact it is benefited. Our souls progress and benefit through every good deed we perform, whether in life or in death.

6

The Power of Creation

There are three types of power. Power of Creation, Power of Maintenance and Power of Destruction. Lord Shiva the Trimurti (fig - 1) represents the power of creation by Lord Brahma, and the power of maintenance by Lord Vishnu, and power of destruction by Lord Shiva (Mahesh). These three powers are the manifestation of the supreme reality in this world. In fact, these three powers are inseparable, in other words, they are only three facets of the same power. There can be more creation without destruction, nor destruction without creation. For example, when the morning is dead, noon is born, when evening is dead night is born and so on. In this chain of births and deaths, creation and destruction, the day is maintained. If we split the word God, G - Growth, O - Observer and D - Destruction, explains the supreme power of God.

To indicate this inseparable nature of creation and destruction Siva the Lord of destruction, has been represented by the organ of procreation.

The source of creation from the nature, by the nature, or God functioning within, or from your five senses you can feel that the God is with in you. The question is whether you can see the God or not, feel His presence or not. The spiritual person can feel His presence within himself and with in everything and around every moment.

When we say God, or soul, Atma or Paramatma, we are talking about the basis of Physical creation. This dimension cannot be perceived through our five senses, yes, we can achieve through our karma. The karma is of many kinds, different layers and dimensions. As I have discussed in depth in my previous book **"Life Before Death"** *ISBN - 978-81-7533-314-7* based on 'Bhagavad Gita'

MAHESH The Annihilator | **VISHNU** The Sustainer | **BRAHMA** The Creator

I have attempted to carry out research, but am ignorant of my basic senses. We need to accept the fact that ultimately, the perfect knowledge stems from the learning enumerated in the following quote from the "**Bhagavad Gita**"

Sanskrit Shloka:

Om ajnana-timirandhasy jnananjana-salakaya
Caksur unmilitam yena tasmai sri-gurave namah

This means: - "I was born in the darkest ignorance, and my spiritual master opened my eyes with the torch of knowledge. I offer my respectful obeisances unto him.

Sanskrit Shloka:-

Purnamadah Purnamidam Purnatpurnam Udachyate,
Purnasya Purnamadaya, Purnameva Vashishyate

This means: - This is perfect, that is perfect and from the perfect, the perfect emerges. If perfect is deducted from the perfect remains.

Sanskrit Shloka:-

"Sahanavavtu Sahanabhunkty Sahaveeryam Karavavahai,
Tejeswina Wadhitamastu ma Vidvishavahai
om, shanti, shanti, shanti!"

This means: -Let Him protect us both, we be blessed with the bliss of knowledge Let us do the brave act together May our studies be thorough and faithful. May we not ever misunderstand each other Oh: Eternity: Peace: Peace: Peace.

The last two lines are a warning towards the possible lack of accuracy and thoroughness of 'the Generalist". Also, the lack of communication results in misunderstanding or misapplication of information or knowledge to design.

Thorough understanding, right application and meaningful communication are important. To get a perfect result it is better to put correct question than to give correct answer to a wrong question.

As I learn, study and get experience staying with the multi - religious society, the truth of all religions, I would like to share with you. The views expressed in this book are strictly personal and do not reflect any body's opinion. First of all I would like to strongly mention that I respect equally all the religions, present on this earth planet.

We are a multi-religious society and that is our strength. All religions provide us with character enhancing traits. We will benefit from integrating these into a common belief system that makes us more humane, more accepting of difference and more sensitive to the plight of others not as fortunate as us.

Thus make a universal secular society, the rise of the conscience does not need a specific time. It is within our capacity to allow this to happen. Religion, spiritualism, morality, faith, truth, world peace, harmony, belief - are just words. We give them power in return, they empower us.

In this world, everyone has to die. When ordinary people die, they undergo all kinds of suffering and pain. But a realized soul's death is different. They die on the day they have realized the self. From that day, they have no attachment to their body. They are ready to leave this human form just as a snake leaves its skin. They only live for the Supreme Brahma who is in them, and for His creation.

In Geeta, the Lord tells Arjun, 'do not consider this body as yours, do not consider worldly possessions to be yours they are all Mine. On this righteous path (the path of Dharma), even if you hurt or kill someone, or do something wrong, I will take the results of those actions on Myself, they will not bind you.'

This is like an ambassador who represents his country in another place. He acts as an agent; his actions are governed by the policies of the nation he represents. If he commits any acts, good or bad, he is not held accountable; his country takes full responsibility for them. He is not praised or punished for them.

That is what Shri Krishna told Arjun. Even if you have to fight this terrible war and kill thousands of people, it will not be a sin. You are fighting for a just cause, without selfish motives. That was the knowledge of the Gita that the Lord gave Arjun on the battlefield of Kurukshetra and made him victorious.

We have several such examples in Indian history, when the men of vision, the realized souls could not be silent spectators to the turbulations in the society and changed the course of history.

In the seventeenth century, the Mughal kings were trying to destroy Hindu religion. They were forcibly converting people, breaking their temples, levying taxes on Hindus, etc. At that time; Saint Ramdas in Maharashtra motivated King Shivaji to fight against the oppressors. Similarly Guru Gobind Singh who was a saint and a warrior, himself led the Sikhs against the Mughal emperor. Mahamati Prannath inspired Maharaja Chhatrasaal to take up arms against the cruel ruler Aurangzeb. He advised him and encouraged him at every step. Not only that, Swamiji gave Maharaja Chhatrasaal as a gift the diamond mines of Panna, which helped him in his battles. All these freedom fighters together made the Mughal Empire weak and it collapsed soon after.

People sometimes feel that once the soul realizes God, then that person becomes useless to society. He just sits in one place all day, praying and chanting the name of the Lord. That is not true. Such a person always has God in his heart. He does not repeat His name whole day. But he continues to act in this world efficiently and successfully. In fact, the quality of his actions improves, because he has no selfish motive he is working for a higher ideal.

A realized soul remembers his beloved Lord at all times whether awake, asleep, talking or working. He always gets supreme joy and bliss. He acts in this world without desire, without attachment. He is not attracted to sense objects. His life is simple and pure. He always works for the benefit of others.

Such a person lives his life like an actor. He knows that his stay on this stage (the world) is brief. He plays his part to the best of his ability. While performing his role, he always remembers his true nature, his real self. He does not forget his true home Paramdham (the Supreme Abode). Such people are true human beings - saints.

Shri Krishna told Arjun that a realized soul always lives in his true nature. Joy or sorrow, praise or blame, they are the same to him that is, he does not get carried away by circumstances. He does not distinguish between friend and foe, he considers everyone to be God's creation. He acts in this world without pride, without a sense of 'doership'. He considers himself as God's representative, His agent. He stays away from the three 'gates of Hell' lust, anger, and pride.

Sanskrit Shloka:-

Tri-vidham marakasyedam
dvaram nasanam atmanah
Kamah krodhas tatha lobhas
tasmad etat trayam tyajet

Bhagavad-gita 16.21

This means: - There are three gates leading to this hell lust, anger and greed. Every sane man should give these up, for they lead to the degradation of the soul.

The beginning of demoniac life is described herein. One tries to satisfy his lust, and when he cannot, anger and greed arises. A sane man who does not want to glide down to the species of demoniac life must try to give up these three enemies, which can kill the self to such an extent that there will be no possibility of liberation from this material entanglement.

7

In Search of Truth

Something is wrong with man himself. Murder, Rape, Theft, Destruction of property. Violence, Crime and Restlessness in the Society, No faith in relationship. Men are running for peace, no faith in each other, everything is out of control.

By this is meant that man clearly does not know how to direct himself. Philosophies, ideas, New Age movements, drugs; all are attempts to find a way to truth. But whosome have believed in this to be the right way have ended in their death. Man is on a sea without direction. This also shows the limitations of man's knowledge. Throughout the world, in all places and all times, men seek for answers?

However, the good side is that there is an awareness, and it is the motivation to seek for answers. The quest for truth can become a prime factor in one's life, and the existence of a myriad of religions and philosophies all testify to this fact. Is the awareness of human inadequacy a design element that the Designer built into the system to motivate man to seek the true answer to life and an understanding of his Creation.

What about all the physical calamities? Can something be both unfortunate and good? Even though something is not working right, if a person is compelled to find out why the system is not working and in so doing they discover a greater good, is it not worthwhile? It's sort of like getting a spanking when you were a kid. Unpleasant, yes! But when you look back you see that its purpose was to lead you into being a more responsible person. The spanking was "unfortunate" but it was also "good." It should also be noted that the spanking reflects an act of justice. It is the penalty for error committed against the authority of the parent.

So, can it be suggested that not only the positive design and goodness seen in nature, but even the negative things are designed to lead men to seek the Creator, because they drive man to find out why this wonderful earth/universe machine is not working properly?

TOWARDS AN ANSWER

First, several things can be established by observation alone. The earth/universe has design; it is "good" and it is directed towards man, but it is also flawed in performance. Something is wrong. Man is trapped in a dark forest without any sure pathway to the light, and the Designer seems far from us and silent.

Second, an explanation is needed; something to wrap around these observations and bind them together. This is called a world-view. An inductive study of facts cannot, by itself, give a world-view. A world view is based on faith and founded on facts. Everyone has a world view. Some include the idea of a Creator and some do not. Not all that include a Creator or biblical world-views. So why do men like John Clayton choose a biblical world view? The answer is that it satisfactorily explains all known observations better than any other.

Third, we as humans are "outside-the-garden" of peoples. We are, in fact, separated from a friend who was once close to us.

Religious belief can result from man seeing design in nature and inferring the existence of a Supreme Designer.

Many see the "good" directed towards man, and conclude that the Designer cares for man. The fact that things have gone wrong in this world testify that there is a problem, and this drives many more to seek answers. The world view expressed that all the observable facts together lead into the most reasonable and consistent pattern.

We are taught so much within our schools, for those of us who have been enrolled in Jewish day schools, high schools and perhaps have attended seminars as well. We become very involved in trying to resolve contradictions between one place in the text and another; we are interested in technicalities and words, literary techniques and laws, and as we focus on these specifics we lose sight of the reason we are doing all this for God. We are taught everything in our schools-except about God.

I think that in some way we must redirect our goals, not in any foolish sense of the word-I am not recommending the institution of a God but simply within our own minds, hearts, and souls. The reason we are here is because of God, and our every action is committed for Him, in order to walk in His ways and to earn the title of His servant. And so it lies upon us to search for God, to strive to find Him, to search for Him and seek Him, to realize that no matter the method or the approach that is used; this is precisely what our brethren desire to do as well. We do it in very different ways and utilize very different methods, but in the end our role is the same-we are all children of God, and it is upon us all to find Him, and to live our lives by walking alongside Him, and desiring to know Him.

Therefore be imitators of God as dear children. And walk in love, he has given Himself for us, an offering and a sacrifice to God for a sweet-smelling aroma. But fornication and all uncleanness or covetousness, must not even be named among you, as is fitting for saints; neither filthiness, nor foolish talking, nor coarse jesting, which are not fitting, but rather giving of thanks. For this you know, that no fornicator, unclean person, nor covetous man, who is an idolater, has any inheritance in the kingdom of God.

Let no one deceive you with empty words, for because of these things the wrath of God comes upon the sons of disobedience. Therefore do not be partakers with them. For you were once in darkness, but now you are in light of the Lord. Walk as children of light (for the fruit of the Spirit is in all goodness, righteousness, and truth), finding out what is acceptable to the Lord. And have no fellowship with the unfruitful works of darkness, but rather expose them. For it is shameful even to speak of those things which are done by them in secret.

But all things that are exposed are made manifest by the light, for whatever makes manifest is light. Therefore He says: "Awake, you who sleep, Arise from the dead, And he will give you light." See then that you walk circumspectly, not as fools but as wise, redeeming the time, because the days are evil. Therefore do not be unwise, but understand what the will of the Lord is.

The soul of man is the sun by which his body is illumined, and from which it draweth its sustenance, and should be so regarded.

The soul not only continues to live after the physical death of the human body, but is, in fact, immortal.

Know thou of a truth that the soul, after its separation from the body, will continue to progress until it attaineth the presence of God, in a state and condition which neither the revolution of ages and centuries, nor the changes and chances of this world, can alter. It will endure as long as the Kingdom of God, His sovereignty, His dominion and power will endure.

In commenting on the immortality of the rational soul, 'Abdu'l- Baha explained that everything in creation which is composed of elements is subject to decomposition:

The soul is not a combination of elements, it is not composed of many atoms, it is of one indivisible substance and therefore eternal. It is entirely out of the order of the physical creation; it is immortal!

Bahá'u'lláh taught that individuals have no existence previous to their life here on earth. Neither is the soul reborn several times in different bodies. He explained, rather, that the soul's evolution is always towards God and away from the material world. A human being spends nine months in the womb in preparation for entry into this physical life. During that nine-month period, the fetus acquires the physical tools (e.g., eyes, limbs, and so forth) necessary for existence in this world. Similarly, this physical world is like a womb for entry into the spiritual world. Our time here is thus a period of preparation during which we are to acquire the spiritual and intellectual tools necessary for life in the next world.

The crucial difference is that, whereas physical development in the mother's womb is involuntary, spiritual and intellectual development in this world depend strictly on conscious individual effort:

The incomparable Creator has created all men from same substance, and hath exalted their reality above the rest of His creatures. Success or failure, gain or loss, must, therefore, depend upon man's own exertions. The more he striveth, the greater will be his progress.

The Bahá'í writings often speak of the bounty or grace of God towards humanity, and explain that an appropriate human response is always necessary for God's grace and mercy to penetrate the human soul and bring about any genuine change within us: "No matter how strong the measure of Divine grace, unless supplemented by personal, sustained and intelligent effort, it cannot become fully effective and be of any real and abiding advantage." Thus, in the Bahá'í conception, salvation is not simply a unidirectional gift from

God to us, but is rather a dialogue, a collaborative venture initiated by God but requiring vigorous and intelligent human participation.

Since human nature is spiritual, the essential capacities of women and men are the capacities of the soul. In other words, one's personality, one's basic intellectual and spiritual faculties, reside in the soul, even though they are expressed through the instrumentality of the body for the short duration of earthly life. Some of the faculties that Bahá'u'lláh mentioned as capacities of the soul are:-

1. The mind, which represents the capacity for rational thought and intellectual investigation;
2. The will, which represents the capacity for self-initiated action; and
3. The "heart or the capacity for conscious, deliberate, self-sacrificing love (sometimes called altruism).

The Bahá'í teachings confirm that the soul retains its individuality and consciousness after death, and is able to associate with other souls that are drawn together by love.

WHY YOUNG PEOPLE HAVE TO DIE ?

In this fast life every day you hear about an accident. I passed the most tragic car accident. It was tragic because a young man was dead behind the steering wheel. I prayed for his soul and family, and later that evening I realized that there are people who die in airplane accidents that look horrific, but some walk away alive, intact with perhaps a few scratches.

I had a deep yearning to learn the truth about death. I asked God, "Why do young people have to die?" The question came from the bottom of my heart.

The following is the answer: -

"You are viewing death as if it is some kind of ending, when in actuality it is merely a new experience in the life of one's soul."

Sanskrit Shalok:

jatasya hi dhruvo mrtyur
dhruvam janma mrtasya ca
tasmad apariharye' rthe
na tvam socitum arhasi

***Bhagavad-gita* 2.27**

> **This means: -** One who has taken his birth is sure to die, and after death one is sure to take birth again. Therefore, in the unavoidable discharge of your duty, you should not lament.

One has to take birth according to one's activities of life. And after finishing one term of activities, one has to die to take next birth. In this way one is going through one cycle of birth and death after another without liberation. This cycle of birth death does not, however, support unnecessary murder, slaughter and war. But at the same time, violence and war are inevitable factors in human society for keeping law and order.

All conscious beings have eternal life. It is the soul of a person that is their life force. The soul desires to have new experiences, or there are younger souls who make a choice of their own free will to enter into physical life for a short time, and their passing would be a catalyst for much needed change and transformation.

I want you to view death as a choice to live in another area or realm. For this is what the soul actually does; it lives in another realm as non-physical soul energy.

Society has created great misunderstandings over death. Far too many people are suffering, and they are suffering because they miss the person they love.

I would like to give you an analogy that may help many people.

If the person you love, has moved to an island which is

without communication, you would still miss that person, and you would adjust to being without him physically.

Even if you never saw him again in this lifetime, you would honor his choice to move into a new way of life.

For many people, death is a new chance for a new beginning. Perhaps they would rather incarnate into a new life rather than stay in their current life.

The people who "die" in terms of how society views death are free of pain. They feel peaceful. Perhaps they feel peace for the first time in many years or decades. They are no longer living in their old life. They simply moved on.

When someone passes, you loved, he is dearly missed by his loved ones, no matter what their chronological age was on the last day of their physical life.

Whether someone was twelve, twenty two, or eighty two, the feelings of missing that person are what the pain is all about. As I shared with you, physical death is moving into a new life.

The people who are left behind so to speak are the one's who suffer, and this suffering can be transformed by sharing a new perspective for anyone who needs it.

The saying, "he passed on" is much more accurate. A person of any age 'passes on' into his new experience of life.

Let me ask you to consider how long you would prefer to remain in this life as you are. Some of you would want to "check out" today. Some others feel they have a mission to complete and then they can 'move on' with a peaceful and fulfilled heart.

The reason you see people escape what look like lethal accidents is simply because it was not their time to move on.

Your life is like a lease, and when the lease is up, it is then time to move on and go back.

Changing houses, countries or lifetimes are very similar

in the actual course of a person's life. If you cannot see or have a back and forth conversation with a loved one who moved away, how is this different from 'passing on'?

Sanskrit Shalok:

dehino' smin yatha dehe
kaumaram yauvanam jara
tatha dehantara-praptir
dhiras tatra na muhyati

Bhagavad-gita: 2.13

This means: - As the embodied soul continuously passes, in this body, from boyhood to youth to old age, the soul similarly passes into another body at death. A sober person is not bewildered by such a change.

Since every living entity is an individual soul, each is changing his body every moment, manifesting sometimes as a child, sometimes as a youth and sometimes as an old man. Yet the same spirit soul is there and does not undergo any changes with the body at death and transmigrates to another body; and since it is sure to have another body in the next birth either material or spiritual.

Truly there is no difference. It is how you are perceiving death. Yes, a physical life came to a finish, and the person's soul moves into a new life and can stay in a new life for as long as they choose. Some people choose eternity on the other side. Some choose a very short time if they want to come back into a new life.

View it as "leasing experiences for the soul." No matter what realm, if the person is in physical form, non-physical form, or a new physical form, the experiences are transitory, but life is eternal.

Sanskrit Shalok:

na jayate mriyate va kadacin
nayam bhutva bhavita van a bhuyah

ajo nityah sasvato' yam purano
na aníllate hanyamane sarire

***Bhagavad-gita* 2.20**

> **This means: -** for the soul there is neither birth nor death at any time. He has not come into being, does not come into being, and will not come into being. He is unborn, eternal, ever-existing and primeval. He is not slain when the body is slain.

Qualitatively, the small atomic fragmental part of the supreme spirit is one with the supreme. He undergoes no changes like the body. The body is subject to six kinds of transformations. It takes its birth from the womb of the mother's body, remains for some time, grows, produces some effects, gradually dwindles, and at last vanishes into oblivion. The soul, however, does not go through such changes. The soul is not born, but, because he takes on a material body, the body takes its birth. The soul does not take birth there, and the soul does not die. Anything which has birth also has death. And because the soul has no birth, it therefore has no past, present or future. It is eternal, ever-existing and primeval, that is, there is no trace in history of his coming into being. Under the impression of the body, we seek the history of birth, etc., of the soul. The soul does not at any time become old, as the body does. The so-called old man, therefore, feels himself to be in the same spirit as in his childhood or youth. The changes of the body do not affect the soul. The soul does not deteriorate like a tree. The soul has no byproduct either. The by-products of the body, namely children, are also different individual souls; and, owing to the body, they appear as children of a particular man. The body develops because of the soul's presence, but the soul has neither offshoots nor change. Therefore, the soul is free from the six changes of the body.

All this is destined to prior to this life. But once incarnated, people 'forget' about the agreements they made on the conscious level. Many people feel a sense of purpose or destiny, they remember their soul's mission for entering into this life to begin with.

It is not, "Why do young people have to die?"

Each soul has a purpose. So many times change and transformation in society are the result of things that happen to people just prior to their passing away, whether it is against Drunk Driving or safety precautions.

Intersections that need safety stop lights, school zones that need a slow speed limit. The list is as endless as life itself. All of these changes were catalyzed by the passing of a loved one to ensure that no one else would pass in that manner again.

This is the decision of the remaining loved ones, and all parties agreed to make this difference prior to entering into this life.

Many parents whose sons and daughters passed on while serving in the military, feel that their child was a hero/ heroine and this is truth. Their child fought to ensure eternal freedom for millions of people, and they knew that their passing had great meaning, just as their physical life did, and just as their eternal life does in non-physical form.

I guide to, the reader, to ask what transformation can be catalyzed as a result of a hero who sacrificed any part of life, at any age. Perhaps someone has grand parent who passes away from any number of causes. Their children and loved ones ensure to keep their memory alive, even if they passed on at what is viewed as an older chronological age.

The life span of a soul is eternal. There is never an end to life. If you are alive, there is a deep needed reason for it. If you love someone who has passed away, there was a deep need for transformation, and this is what I would like you to focus on.

Sanskrit Shalok:

nainam chindanti sastrani
nayam dahati pavakah
na cainam kledayanty apo
na sosayati marutah

***Bhagavad-gita* 2.23**

This means: - the soul can never be cut to pieces by any weapon, nor burned by fire, nor moistened by water, nor withered by the wind.

All kinds of weapons like swords, flame weapons, rain weapons, tornado weapons, etc. are unable to kill the soul. It appears that there were many kinds of weapons made of earth, water, air, ether, etc., in addition to the modern weapons of fire. Even the nuclear weapons of the modern age are classified as fire weapons, but formerly there were other weapons made of all different types of material elements. Fire weapons were counteracted by water weapons, which are now unknown to modern science, nor do modern scientists have knowledge of tornado weapons. Nonetheless, the soul can never be cut into pieces, nor annihilated by any number of weapons, regardless of scientific devices.

You come into a transient life, with agreements to transform, and then you change form when you transfer from physical to non-physical life. Do you see a correlation here?

Generally it is said that every one comes on this planet empty handed & goes empty handed after death. But I have changed this theory. When a child is born, he takes birth with both hand totally closed tightly, as he is holding some very important thing in his hands , and when a person passes away, his both hands are empty & open, whether he dies natural death or unnatural death.

So my argument is that he held a very important thing in his both hands, in one hand he held a return ticket duly confirmed, stamped, non-transferable, and on his other hand he brought his privious birth balance sheet (Karma). When he passed away he did not take away any materialistic thing but with him he takes his present Karma the duty, true and sincere services he has rendered during his life time towards his parents, Guru, and the society he was living with and the contribution he has earned towards his religion and his country for his next birth.

Whether this has helped you, is, determined by how you are viewing the soul you love who has moved or transferred into a new life, on the other side, and has the universe of possibilities to return in order to create new transformations. This cycle is called reincarnation.

Just as people have had many lives, there are also many reasons a person chooses to come into this life, as well as when, why and how to pass into the next life. Please view all souls as eternally alive. If you are missing someone who died, call out his name. They can hear you. Your loved one can visit you, and it is just a short time in terms of the age of the universe when you share the company of a loved one again. But do not take your own life.

Choosing to take your life will only cause you to come right back and complete the mission you signed up for. Please know that eternal life is for every soul. The life of the soul is eternal. The love you share with anyone is eternal. The passing of a loved one, or anyone, is filled with meaning and that meaning was one of the reasons they came into this life.

Death is not an end at all. It is a new beginning in the life experiences of the soul. Please remember that.

Sanskrit Shalok:

vasamsi jirnani yatha vihaya
navani grhanati naro' parani
tatha sarirani vihaya jirnany
anyani samyati navani dehi

Bhagavad-gita: - 2: 22

This means: - As a person puts on new garments, giving up old ones, the soul similarly accepts new material bodies, giving up the old and useless ones.

Change of body by the atomic individual soul is an accepted fact. Even the modern scientists who do not believe in the existence of the soul, but at the same time cannot explain the source of energy from the heart, have to accept continuous changes of body which appear from childhood to boyhood and from boyhood to youth and again from youth to old age. From old age, the change is transferred to another body. This has already been explained in my previous book - **A Practical guide to an Ageless Mind Spiritual Laws of Vedic Philosophy.**

ISBN: - 81-900614-3-7.

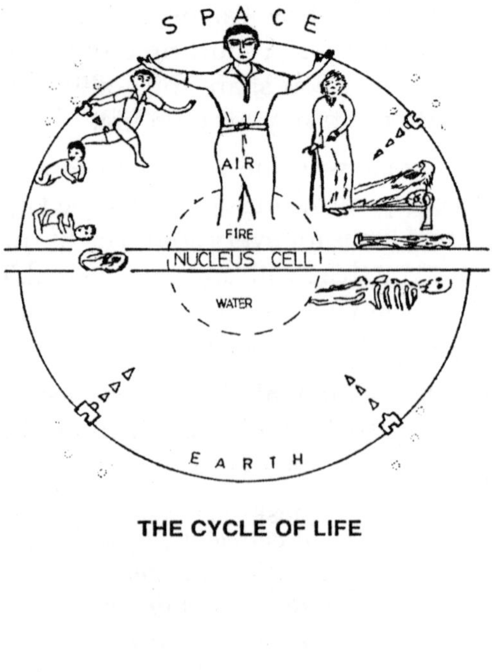

THE CYCLE OF LIFE

8

Composition of Man (Inner Engineering)

Man is constituted of the supreme self and the body mind intellect equipment. Self is the Spirit, called Atman. The body mind intellect is matter, composed of the five elements of nature viz. space, air, fire, water and earth. The physical body is made up of gross elements. Mind and intellect are made up of subtle elements. These three equipments are inert and insentient. But when these equipments come in contact with Atman they gain sentiency. Atman is the sentient-principle, the life-giving force or power. Atman is related to body-mind-intellect just as electricity is to an electric bulb in itself has no light. Nor does electricity, but when electricity contacts the bulb there is a brilliant expression of light. Similarly, body, mind and intellect have no life inherent in them. Nor does Atman, But when Atman combines with body-mind-intellect there is a scintillating expression of life.

The physical body houses the five organs of perception and the five organs of action. The organs of perception take in stimuli from the external world. The organs of action send out responses after the stimuli have reacted with the mind-and-intellect.

The mind receives the stimuli through the sense organs

of perception. The five senses send in different stimuli such as colour and form, sound, smell, taste and touch. Mind gains an integrated experience of them all. The function of the intellect is to examine stimuli and decide on the type of response to be sent out through the organs of action. Mind may be compared to a clerk receiving mail in a business organization. Intellect will then be the officer directing disposal of the mail. If the clerk were to answer the mail himself the organization will subject itself to irresponsible action. Such an organization will collapse ultimately. Similarly, if your mind responds to stimuli without the guidance of the intellect you will lead yourself to a disastrous end. This is the fate of a man who acts on mere impulses. Whereas a man who uses his intellectual discrimination to guide his actions is bound to be successful and progressive in life.

BASIC FIVE SENSES OF MAN AND CORRESPONDING CO-RELATION WITH COSMOS

FIVE SENSES	HEARING	TOUCH	SIGHT	TASTE	SMELL
The basic Elements	**Space**	**Air**	**Fire**	**Water**	**Earth**
Instruments of Perception (To acquire inward)	Ears	Skin	Eyes	Tongue	Nose
Work Organs (To act outward)	Speech Communication	Hands Work (Exit)	Feet Mobility (Finger)	Anus Discard	Genitals Procreate
Control Centre Force	Mind (Flow of Thoughts or Emotions)		Intellect (Power of Discrimination)		
The Presidin Force	The Cosmos Consciossencess or Supreme Energy. ' Prana' or the life force.				
Transforms related Technological Fields)	(a) Silence (b) Acoustics tics	Climate Weather Conditioning	Light Colour	Plumbing Cooling	Landscape Flore
	(c) Vibrations	Texture Surface	Texture forms	Repose/ Reflection	Odour

The material components viz. body, mind and intellect are enlivened by Soul. Soul is therefore the life-principle or God-principle within you. Atman is another word of God. It is that transcendental power which vitalizes your body to act and perceive your mind to feel and your intellect to think. Without the life-principle in you, your body, mind and intellect cannot function. They remain inert like the mass of matter around you.

Your physical body, mind and intellect are constantly changing. You recognize the changes occurring in them. But according to science a change is noticeable only with reference to a changeless factor. In the absence of a changeless entity you do not recognize changes taking place. You experience this scientific truth when you are flying in an aircraft in a cloudless sky. You do not notice the movement of the plane at all since there are no unmoving fixtures around. Therefore your cognizance of the physical, mental and intellectual changes posits the existence of an unchanging factor within you. This changeless entity in you is Atman.

Furthermore you refer to your material equipments as 'my body', 'my mind' and 'my intellect'. The interposing of the possessive pronoun 'my' indicates that the possessor (you) is distinct and different from the possessed (body, mind and intellect). Body, mind and intellect are therefore your possessions. They belong to you. Then the question arises-who are you? If you take away these material equipments from your personality there seems nothing left behind. Yet you can conceive an unknown factor integrating these equipments and claiming them as its possessions. This unknown being is your true Self. It is Atman. It is you.

Soul is the core of your personality. It is the prime mover of your three material equipments. But your *vasanas* (inherent tendencies) determine the nature of activities emanating from them. If your *vasanas* are *sattwic* in nature your thoughts, desires and actions will also be *sattwic*. If your *vasanas* are *rajasic* or *tamasic* their manifestations again will be of the same type. If your *vasanas* are of a kind and generous nature your intellectual ideas, your emotional feelings and your physical actions will be kind and generous. If they are cruel and wicked so will be their manifestations. As the vasanas so the thoughts, desires and actions.

Your composite personality is created by Atman functioning in your body, mind and intellect. as explained below : -

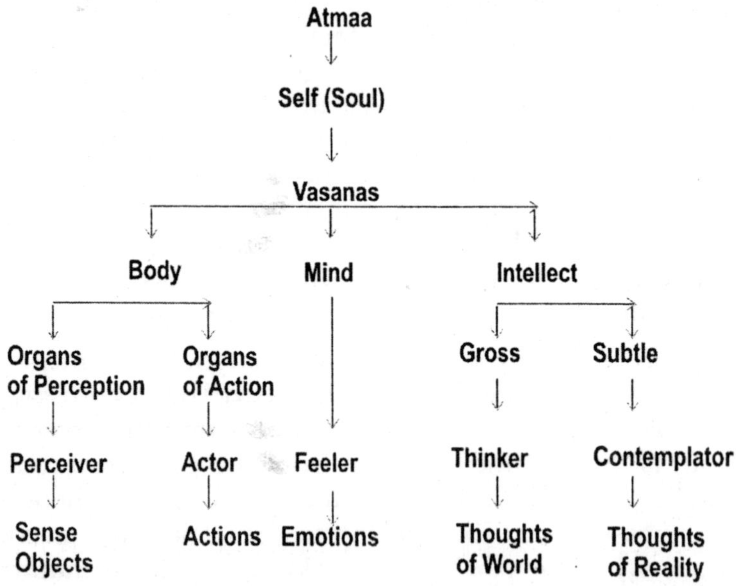

When soul functions in your organs of perception (*gnana indriyas*) you become the 'perceiver'. Perceiver means the combined 'seer-hearer-smeller-taster-toucher'. The perceiver in you perceives sense objects of the world. Sense objects perceived are colour and form through eyes, sound through ears, smell through nose, taste through tongue, touch through skin. The perceiver is one part of your physical personality. The other part is the 'actor'. When Atman functions in your organs of action (*karma indriyas*) you become the 'actor'. The actor in you perpetrates your actions in the world. The perceiver-cum-actor is your physical personality.

Again the atman functioning in your mind creates the 'feeler' in you. The feeler is your emotional personality feeling emotions of different sorts.

A.1. Five Reflective instruments of perception (Physical /Mental):	Ears	Skin	Eyes	Tongue	Nose
2.	Accoustics Vibrations	Climatology H.V.A.C Texture Form Visuals	Lighting Colour	Water supply	Appropriate smells to Aesthetic related activities
B.1. Five universal Activities	Communicate	Work	Movements	Discard	General
2. Reflective Work Organs (Physical)	Speech	Hands	Legs	Anus	Genitals
3. Environmental Transfers	Design Language Systems Special	Function Efficiency systems	Circulations systems	Sewerage (Judiciary)	Generative Systems
C.1. The Mind or Energy	Energy	Emotional	Intellectual	Vital	Blissful
2. Transfers	Non-Measurable Dimensions Depicting Mental Comforts	Ego	Culture	Time	Space Form

We shall elaborately deal each one of these natural elements.

The same atman functioning in your gross intellect is the 'thinker', your intellectual personality. Human intellect is of two distinct types i.e. gross and subtle intellects. When your intellect engages its discriminating faculty in the realm of the terrestrial world it is said to be 'gross'. Gross intellect thinks of thoughts pertaining to the world.

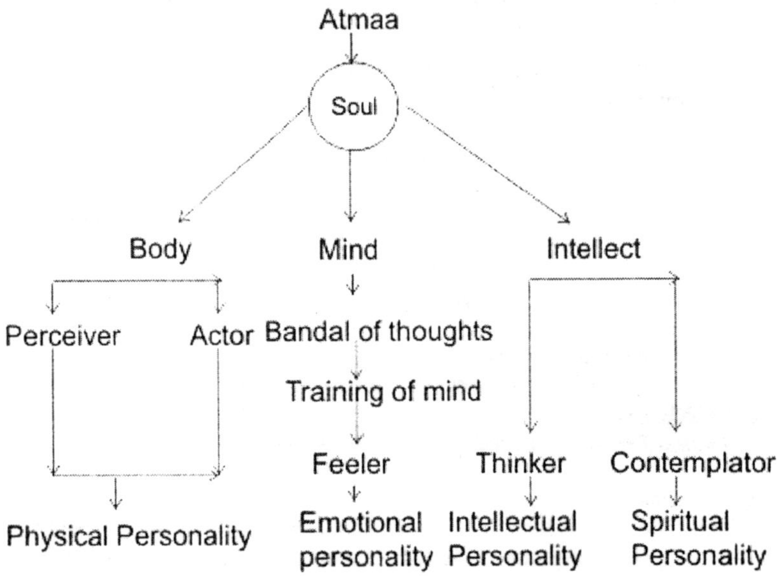

It discriminates between the pairs of opposites all within the boundary of a dog between its master and a stranger to the finest discrimination of a scientist in nuclear technology. But all of them are still classified as gross by virtue of its field of operation being the terrestrial world. When however your intellect crosses the boundary of the terrestrial world and conceives the possibility of a transcendental reality it is called 'subtle' intellect.

No other creature except a human being can posit the transcendental reality. The subtle intellect is the discriminating faculty which contemplates upon and distinguishes the transcendental reality from the terrestrial world, discerns the difference between spirit and matter, between Atman and the world you experience through your material equipments.

When Atman functions in your subtle intellect, you become the 'contemplator'. The contemplator revels in the thought of Atman, Brahman, God, transcendental Reality, supreme Consciousness or whatever name you give it. The contemplator distinguishes between Atman and the worlds of waking, dream and deep-sleep. The contemplator in you is your spiritual personality as explained above.

Your Atman appears as an individual. Atman is omnipresent. It is like the sun whose rays are all pervading. There is just one sun above. But wherever there is reflecting surface there appears in it a reflected sun, an individual sun. The reflected sun assumes the properties of the reflecting medium.

The sun seen through a blue mirror appears blue. The sun seen through a dirty mirror appears dirty, through a broken mirror, broken and so on. But the sun above is immaculate and unconditioned by the qualities of the reflecting media. Similarly there is just one all-pervading Atman. But wherever there is a body-mind-intellect equipment Atman appears through it as an individual human being. The individual takes to the properties of his body, mind and intellect but not Atman. Atman remains ever pure and uncontaminated like the sun vis-à-vis its images.

Atman is also referred to as the unconditioned pure consciousness. When the pure consciousness functions through the body it is conscious of perceptions and actions. The unconditioned consciousness becomes 'conditioned consciousness'. Consciousness conditioned by the body is the physical personality. Similarly consciousness functioning through the mind is conscious of its emotions and becomes the emotional personality.

Thus the individual comprising the four personalities is produced by the conditioning of the pure consciousness by the physical body, mind and intellect. This phenomenon is like the image produced by the reflection of the sun in a mirror. When the mirror is removed there is no longer a reflection. Similarly when the body, mind and intellect conditioning is removed the individual is no more.

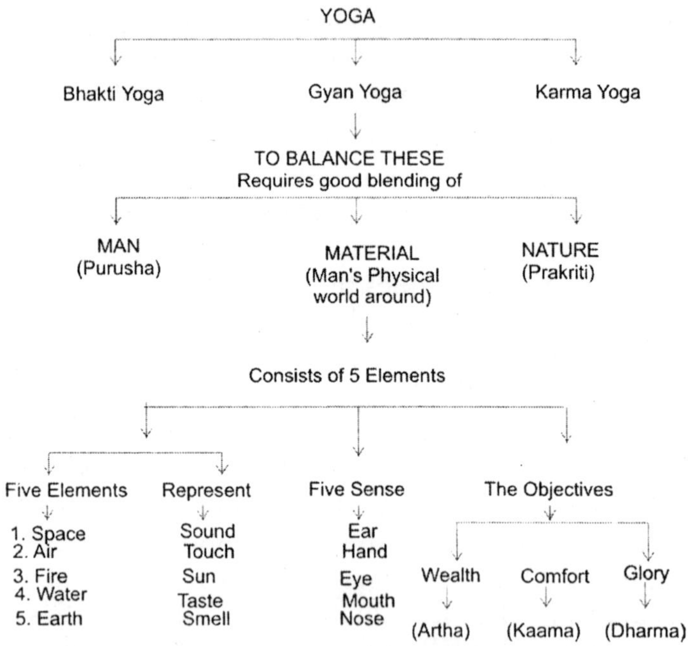

What remains is the unconditioned, pure Consciousness. When the objects of consciousness i.e. your perceptions, actions, emotions and thoughts are clean dropped, you can no longer be conscious of anything. You regain your original state i.e. absolute consciousness. The conditioning of consciousness is brought about by your unintelligent identification and attachment to your body, mind and intellect. Such identification and attachment is removed by following the path of action (karma yoga) with the help of your body, by path of devotion (bhakti yoga) with your mind and by path of knowledge (gyan yoga).

Sanskrit Shalok:

Naiva kincit karomiti
yukto manyeta tattva-vit
Pasyan srnvan spran jighrann
asnan gachan svapan svasan
Pralapan visrian grhnann
unmisan nimisann api
indriyanindriyarthesu
vartanta iti dharayan

***Bhagavad-gita:* - 5. 8-9**

This means: - A person in the divine consciousness, although engaged in seeing, hearing, touching, smelling, eating, moving about, sleeping and breathing, always knows within himself that he actually does nothing at all. Because while speaking, evacuating, receiving, or opening or closing his eyes, he always knows that only the material senses are engaged with their objects and that he is aloof from them.

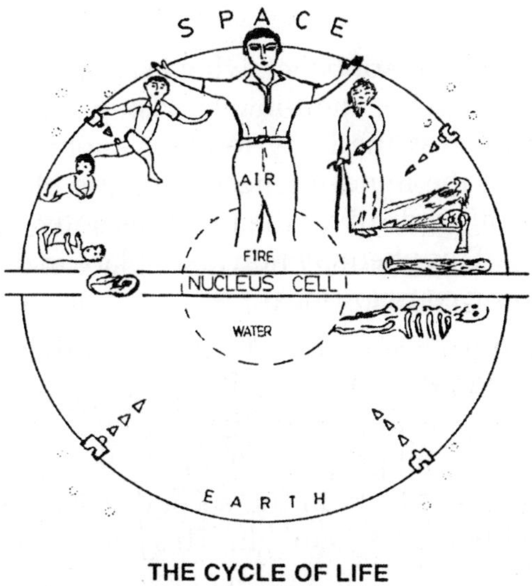

THE CYCLE OF LIFE

With your intellect pure consciousness is all-pervading. Being so it is immovable. Anything that is omnipresent, all-pervading cannot move. An object can move from a place 'where it is' to a place 'where it is not'. If it is everywhere then there is no place 'where it is not'. How then can it move? Where can it move? Therefore anything that is all pervading cannot move. So it is with Atman. Yet the general belief is that Atman moves away from the physical body when a person dies.

Sanskrit Shalok:

dehino' smin yatha dehe
kaumaram yauvanam jara
tatha dehantara-praptir
dhiras tatra na muhyati

Bhagavad-gita: 2.13

> **This means: -** As the embodied soul continuously passes, in this body, from boyhood to youth to old age, the soul similarly passes into another body at death. A sober person is not bewildered by such a change.

As per my theory or belief, what exactly happens at the time of death is that the mind-intellect along with its inherent vasanas Soul leaves the body to enter another body. The transference of the mind-intellect from one physical body to another is called death of the previous body and birth of the new body. This phenomenon takes place in the medium of all-pervading consciousness.

When a mirror is removed from one frame and fixed in another frame the reflected sun which appeared in the mirror in the first frame now shifts to the mirror in the second frame. For all purposes the reflected sun is dead in the first frame and born in the second. It happens in the medium of all-pervading sunlight. This phenomenon cannot take place if sunlight is not present everywhere. Atman is like the all-pervading sunlight. The mind-intellect is like the mirror in the frame of the physical body.

To tread the spiritual path you will have to gear your inner mechanism properly. Your body senses and mind should follow the dictates of your subtle intellect. You will then reach your desired destination. If not, your senses become uncontrollable, your body gets damaged and your mind agitated. You meet disaster.

This whole idea is well portrayed in the picture of the chariot with Arjuna in it and Lord Krishna as charioteer. The horses of the chariot are strong and powerful but they are kept under perfect control. The charioteer holds them firmly with the help of the reins. The horses represent your senses, chariot your body, reins your mind and charioteer your intellect. If the charioteer inattentive, the reins go loose, the horses rush helter-skelter. Instead of taking the chariot to its proper destination the horses destroy it along with its occupant. You will likewise meet with disaster if your intellect does not maintain its control over your mind and senses.

Sanskrit Shalok:

Sarva-dvaresu dehe' smin
prakasa upajayate
jnanam yada tada vidyad
vivrddham sattvam ity uta

Bhagavad-gita: 14.11

This means: - The manifestation of the mode of goodness can be experienced when all the gates of the body are illuminated by knowledge.

There are nine gates in the body: two eyes, two ears, two nostrils, the mouth, the genitals and the anus. When every gate is illuminated by the symptoms of goodness, it should be understood that one has developed the mode of goodness. In the mode of goodness, one can see things in the right position, one can hear things in the right position, and one can taste things in the right position. One becomes cleansed inside and outside, in every gate there is development of the symptoms of happiness, and that is the position of goodness.

9

Selfless Service

It is said that the performance of service is one of the methods by which we can achieve glory in the eyes of God. Bhai Gur Das has gone so far as to say that our hands and feet are useless if they perform no service. And Guru Nanak has stated that a person engaged in selfless service is always highly esteemed in the society of men as well as in the eyes of God.

Cheerfully carrying out the orders of elders and rendering them physical help for their comfort and convenience is one phase of service. Another phase of it is rendering loving help to the poor and the needy.

The reward of selfless service is great indeed. The saying goes: "Render service and reap the fruit thereof." Human beings can even become saints and swamis through service.

If we render service with an ulterior motive or with pride and arrogance, we are deprived of its real reward. But if we perform service without any desire for reward we can attain great heights.

Those who render no service to mankind cannot hope to achieve anything in this world or the next. One who does not serve his fellow beings is worthless. There are four kinds of services:

1. Service rendered by soul.

2. Physical service rendered with the body
3. Service rendered by mind
4. Service with wealth

O God, I wish to serve the saints
Not only with my hands but also with my eyes
And indeed with every hair of my head,
Which I may use to cleanse the feet of the saints.
At all times of the day and night
I long for the darshan (sight) of the saints.
This is the only bliss for which I yearn.

(Guru Arjun, AG 1217)

I shall sacrifice my body and mind
and burn my ego at the altar of the saints.
I shall do all kinds of menial service for my Master,
and regard as nectar whatever I receive in return.
I am ever prepared to sacrifice myself to my Master
and fall at his feet,
For I am poor and helpless
and am constantly pining for his darshan

(Guru Arjun, AG 757)

You should therefore serve such a person
who perceives the devotion
and the inner longing of your heart.
Such a one is none other than a perfect Master.
You should make an offering of your mind
at the altar of your Guru,
And worship him because he is the incarnation
of that Deathless One.

(Guru Arjun, AG 614)

We are by now aware of the various types of services by the soul. But the soul can render service only through the grace of God. In order to win his grace, we should pray to the saints who are God incarnate. Thus, it is with the grace of the Master that soul is able to render service.

The ability to merge oneself with the Name of God

(Nam, Word or Shabd) is beyond the comprehension of the intellect. It is therefore only through the grace of a Master that the soul can render service. And the Master's grace is invoked when, by means of devotion, the disciple completely renounces his ego.

How can we achieve this? It is possible only when the soul, by means of repetition of the holy names given by the Master, goes within by withdrawing itself from the nine outlets of the body, pierces through the star, the sun and the moon, and beholds the Radiant Form of the Master. It then merges in the Sound and gradually rises by stages till it reaches its final goal. This is the true service by soul.

One who loves the Lord also loves his creation. Thus the fatherhood of God and the brotherhood of man are realized, and in this manner love is developed in us not only for God but also for his creation.

Man has a physical body. He also has a mind and an intellect, as well as a soul. With the body he accumulates wealth and all other physical amenities. Body is served by body, and with the mind is served Brain, with Brain he accumulates knowledge (Gayan) mind is served by Brain. But soul is by far the most precious of the three. And it is a Master who gives us the gift of the knowledge of the soul. That is why a person should offer his body, his wealth and his mind to the Master.

10

Paths are Different, God is One

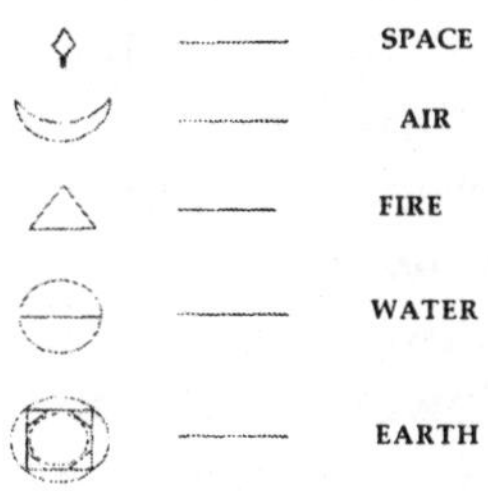

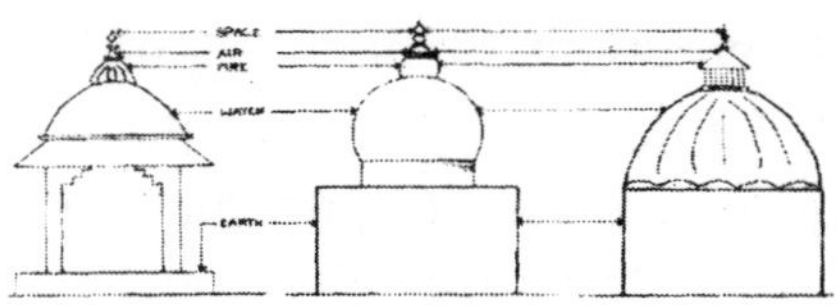

Amazing fact: - they all are same: -

MANDIR = 6 words

CHURCH = 6 words

MASJID = 6 words

GEETA = 5 words

BIBLE = 5 words

QURAN = 5 words

Perhaps the religious beliefs given to me by my parents in my childhood gave me a deep faith in religion. The constant coming of great souls to the house, the association with religious heads and the respect and attraction of my father and mother towards religion gave me a strong faith in God from my very childhood. From then I started enjoying religious congregations, assemblies and the words of great spiritual souls and with age, my perseverance and curiosity increased. Religious gatherings, assemblies and congregations constantly attracted me for in such programs I always felt a great spiritual joy.

As my curiosity increased I wanted to know about and understand other religions besides my own. I wanted to know why the Supreme Power is one, whereas religions are separate. What is the difference between them? Why is there so much opposition? Many such questions arose in my mind. On studying different religions, I found that basically there is no difference of opinion or opposition in accepting the Supreme Power, but the elaboration of the concept of this Supreme Power is different in each religion. All accept the Supreme Power, but the method of knowing, of accepting its form, the methods of reaching Him and worshipping Him are different. The basic thing is the same and in the fundamentals there are no differences.

As I understand, the creator of the entire universe is one; He is One Power, One Light, One Consciousness, One Strength and One Authority. Whether we sing praises to his abstract form or we worship him in his manifested form; whether we salute the nameless one in some temple or mosque, or we prostrate ourselves before him; with a true and pure heart, whatever be our belief, if we call him, worship him or bow before him, our prayers reach the same Illumined Beauty. Just as in different countries and in different societies the modes of addressing the father are different Bapu, Papa, Daddy, or Abba they all mean the same thing. Similarly, despite different concepts of the form of God and different modes of addressing him as well as different places and modes of worship, that Divine Beauty is one. The different religions and sects are only different paths of reaching him. Just as all rivers become one with the ocean, all religions, too, take us towards God.

From the point of view of religion both people and society can be divided into two distinct categories: those who believe in God and, those who do not i.e, believers and non-believers. If efforts are made to awaken religious consciousness and faith in God in such non-believers then it would be like lighting a lamp in the darkness, facilitating the spiritual upliftment of mankind.

The majority of societies and people of the world follow some religion or the other. Through different points of view, they accept the supreme power of God. The majority worship God though in different ways. In order to get to know our supreme father, God, we must have faith in religion though we worship him through the different rites and rituals of various sects and religions which we inherit from our mother and father at birth.

Our religions and paths are different but goal is the same. All religions and sects take us towards that very God, our Supreme father. If all paths take us towards the same goal, then which path is superior and which inferior? All roads that lead in the same direction are equal and great; we may choose whichever religion we like, but if we give other religions full respect, we will attain our goal with greater ease, because religion is the loving means of bringing man closer to man, the beneficent means of the good of mankind.

I am of the opinion that faith in God leads to world peace, happiness and prosperity. Religion, therefore, must be followed but to compel anyone to convert or to give inducement for conversion or to have this agenda is not good.

All religions speak of human welfare. The Sanatan Dharma, for instance, goes to the extent of declaring that they are secular and universal.

The Holy Bible maintains also: -

'Love your enemies and pray for those who trouble you'

The Holy Koran asserts:-

'Good and evil are not similar. You return evil with good. Thus even if there was animosity between you and another, he will become your close friend'.

What a similarity is there in all these lines taken from different texts and what harmony of thought!

All religions are great. All religions teach man to walk on the path of humanity, and all religions teach mankind to follow human values like truth, love, compassion, non-violence, and benevolence!

Then which religion is superior and which inferior? The root of all religions is the same, only the branches are different. Likewise the boundaries of countries are separate, but the earth is one; people are citizens of different countries, but they are all inhabitants of the same earth. The air, sunshine and the river water or sea has no boundaries. The five element of nature are freely available to all with out any bonding or religions. If we see this then why are the differences? The Creator of this earth and this universe is the same. Where is then the duality? If we are fundamentally the same from every point of view, then the need is to understand this similarity, to propagate it and to accept this truth.

The United Nations is a great organization which has taken the lead in maintaining peace. It has determined the political and geographical boundaries of all nations. If any country violates the borders of another country, the United Nations takes collective action against the violating nation. Similarly, if any religion of the world disregards the religion prevalent in another country or society and tries to initiate the people there into its own religion, then this would be called violence against the religion prevalent in that country.

Today the need is that in order to maintain world peace, the United Nations raise its voice in protest against organized and predetermined plans of conversion and exercise control over them. Organized or pre-determined conversion is a violation of the faith of the people of that religion; it creates distance between the two societies, which is not beneficial to humanity.

Today, voices are being raised for nuclear disarmament and universal brotherhood; in today's world, it would be a pragmatic step to also put a stop to such conversions for world peace. By doing so, the bitterness and distance between different religions and communities will be lessened and the feeling of friendship and brotherhood will develop which will be a permanent and worth while step towards maintenance of world peace. The need today is that the heads and followers of all religions, all intellectuals and philosophers, religious teachers and saints come unitedly forward for universal brotherhood and casting aside their differences, support the prohibition on conversion with one voice.

Today, when the world has entered into twenty-first century, it is necessary to organize a world religious conference in which all the heads and teachers of all the religions of the world participate, in which universal good and establishment of universal peace is discussed and in which while paying obeisance to all religions and accepting all of them as great, a resolution be passed prohibiting conversion. That will be an invaluable religious gift to all humanity.

All religions are equal, all religions are great. This beneficient message should be spread throughout the world.

If there are differences in the various religions, there are also similarities, and if we study the scriptures in depth, we will find that the fundamentals are the same. Basically there are fewer differences and more similarities. Only the vision is needed and the desire to come closer to each other.

Today, when the entire world is aspiring for total disarmament, our efforts to create a climate of goodwill and friendship are also one.

Standing on the threshold of the twenty-first Century, let us get rid of weapons, leave our egos, discard discrimination between big and small, superior and inferior and search for ways, of nearness and equality of love and friendship.

Let us have a new vision and new thoughts for the benefit of humanity.

My aim in writing this book is to establish closeness among the followers of different religions and to emphasize the harmony in the thoughts of various religions, and to attempt to awaken faith among people and societies; to remove the distances between human beings through respect for all religions, to generate feelings of love. If this book can play some role in this direction, I will feel that my attempt has been fruitful.

Religion has changed its form many times in the history of civilization.

Religion has provided man with the kind of spiritual peace without which he cannot even achieve material prosperity. The secret of the prosperity and progress of developed countries is also perhaps their essential core of spirituality and religiosity in its purest sense; not in a narrow way but in a broad pervasive sense. In America the words "**In God we Trust**" are stamped on the official currency, the dollar itself. Countries, which have ignored the spirituality of religion and made it the instrument of politics and propaganda have had to face a variety of problems.

It is in the nature of man that he desires to surrender

before an unknown supreme Power; it is perhaps because his life has more unhappiness than happiness.

The average man cannot become a philosopher who can ponder over the pros and cons of this supreme power and spend his life in arguments for and against it. For the average man, the biggest problem is to maintain his existence. In his life, happiness is elusive. Faith in his religion and unshakable belief in God give him the necessary courage to go ahead in his life; they save him from breakdowns. It is because of this that when in communist countries, in spite of the promise of equality, equal opportunity, material happiness and prosperity, the lives of the majority of the people remained as unhappy as before, that belief in religion and unlimited faith in God gave them strength. Because of restrictions imposed by the authorities, people could not go to public places of worship but in their own hearts and homes, they derived life-giving energy through remembering God.

It is a happy paradox that while on the one hand, man is reaching new peaks of material prosperity, is preparing to land on Mars after having successfully done so on the Moon, he is on the other hand, getting more and more attracted towards spirituality. The landing of man on the Moon was not only the greatest event of the twentieth century but of the history of the human race itself. Although this victory exploded many old postulates and tenets, surprisingly those astronauts who returned after landing on the Moon and encircling it did not become agnostic. They became even more spiritual than before.

The transformation in Neil Armstrong, the first man to land on the Moon and Allen Glen, his partner, bears witness to this truth. In this sense, material prosperity and the ever-new achievements of science are taking us towards spirituality and faith in some Supreme Power. A survey conducted by a magazine in India reveals that 80 to 90 %

youth are moving towards spirituality. They have faith in the philosophies and codes of their religions.

In the blood we can not find the different Religions or different Blood colors or caste, the Soul is also same.

Religion begins where science ends.

11

Inner Joy

For the past few years it seems like each year has been more difficult than the previous one. I have been through a series of trials and discouragements, times when the joy of the Lord has not been in my heart. Through all these trials one lesson has repeatedly been taught: after each trial I appreciate all the more just how precious is the Lord. I have come to identify more closely with the parables, finding that the Lord is indeed like tremendously valuable treasure. There is nothing that is as precious; not money, nor power, nor career advancement, nor popularity. All these pale in front the Lord. Through these trials the Lord has weaned me off the things that I formerly thought precious, the things to which I formerly gave value or weight. The passion that I once had for those things is being turned into a passion for the Lord. I doubt that this would happen without trials.

I have come to believe that it is through trials and sufferings that the Lord teaches us His preciousness. He removed all physical blessings in order to teach us an important spiritual lesson.

Inner joy

The inner joy is if you are happy without any reason. you do not have any reason to be happy but still you are happy is called inner happiness.

God has already given us every spiritual blessing. If we appreciate these spiritual blessings we will realize that mere physical blessings are insignificant. Above all, we will come to rejoice in the greatest gift of all, that God has given us Himself. "How priceless is your unfailing love! Both high and low among men find refuge in the shadow of your wings. They feast on the abundance of your house; you give them drink from your river of delights. For with You, is the fountain of life; in your light we see light"

Sanskrit Shalok:

Yam hi na vyathayanty ete
purusam purusarsabha
sama-duhkha-sukham dhiram
So' mrtatvaya kalpate

Bhagavad-gita: 2.15

This means: - O best among men [Arjuna], the person who is not disturbed by happiness and distress and is steady in both is certainly eligible for liberation.

Anyone who is steady in his determination for the advanced stage of spiritual realization and can equally tolerate the onslaughts of distress and happiness is certainly a person eligible for liberation. In the varnasrama institution, the fourth stage of life, namely the renounced order (sannyasa), is a painstaking situation. But one who is serious about making his life perfect surely adopts the sannyasa order of life in spite of all difficulties. The difficulties usually arise from having severe family relationships, to give up the connection of wife and children, but if anyone is able to tolerate such difficulties, surely his path to spiritual realization is complete.

They say the eyes are windows to the soul. Can

you see mine? No, and I can't see yours. Some folks say they can see auras. I've had people tell me they can see mine. Auras, I guess, are in some way associated with souls but I've never seen one and I don't know that they have seen either.

On the other hand, I could be wrong. I can't prove it after all, one way or another. I can't even prove I have a soul, though I believe I do. I can't prove you have a soul either, given that I can't see it, but I'm willing to grant that if I have one, other people do have too. Of course, some people might not want to have souls, or rather, they don't believe they do because either they don't believe in things they can't see or they don't believe in things like God and soul and an "Other-world." And that's fine. I am sure wouldn't push a soul or a God on anyone.

And science will never be able to nail it down for us because scientifically-speaking, we can't see souls.

The soul, if it chooses, also can suppress the spirit and take some other delight as lord of the man. This trinity of spirit, soul and body may be partially illustrated by a light bulb. Within the bulb, which can represent the total man, there are electricity, light and wire. The spirit is like the electricity, the soul the light, and body the wire. Electricity is the cause of the light while light is the effect of electricity. Wire is the material substance for carrying the electricity as well as for manifesting the light. The combination of spirit and body produces soul, that which is unique to man. As electricity, carried by the wire, is expressed in light, so spirit acts upon the soul and the soul, in turn, expresses itself through the body.

As I have mentioned already, the soul is the meeting-point of spirit and body, for there they are merged. By his spirit man holds intercourse with the spiritual world and with the Spirit of God, both receiving and expressing the power and life of the spiritual realm. Through his body man is in contact with the outside sensuous world, affecting it and being affected by it. The soul stands between these two worlds, yet belongs to both. It is linked with the spiritual world through the spirit and with the material world through the body.

IN THE END I WOULD AGAIN LIKE TO REPEAT, THAT I RESPECT ALL RELIGIONS EQUALLY, BUT BY IGNORANCE IF ANY WAY I HURT ANY BODY'S FEELING, HE OR SHE SHALL NOT TAKE IT SERIOUSLY. MY AIM IN WRITING THIS BOOK, IS TO TELL THE WORLD THAT ALL RELIGIONS ARE EQUAL. NO ONE SHOULD CONSIDER THAT THEIR RELIGION IS SUPERIOR THAN THE OTHER, BECAUSE SOUL IS SAME, GOD IS ONE, BUT PATHS ARE DIFFERENT.

WITH MY BLESSINGS TO ALL THE READERS..

B B Puri
Author

12

Blessings from Spiritual Leaders as I Learn from them

Prof. Puri with H.H. Pilot Baba Ji at Haridwar

Prof . Dr. B. B. Puri taking blessing from Dr. Murli Mahoher Joshi ji Minister for HRD, H.H. Swami Chidanand Saraswati ji and H.H. Gopal Krishan Goswami ji head ISKOCN and other spiritual leader's at International Vedic Conference 2005.

Prof B B Puri having discussion with Late Shri Rajiv Gandhi, Former Prime Minister of India

Prof B B Puri with Smt. Shiela Dixit, Chief Minister, New Delhi

Prof. Puri with Swami Chinmayanand Ji
Minister of State Govt. Of India

Prof. Puri with Shri K. R. Narayanan Former President of India, lighting the Lamp.

Prof. Dr. B.B. Puri with Sadhguru Jaggi Vasudev ji , Shri D.R. Kaarthikeyan and other spiritual leaders at International Vedic Convention "Mind, Body, Soul & Health" 22nd &23rd Oct. 2005

Prof. Puri with Dr. Karan Singh, at International Vedic Convention 2005 "Mind, Body, Soul & Health"

Architect Dr. PURI congratulated for his training of students on Vastu as science Vastu Padmasri Kalaimamani Sir Dr. S. RAMAN "SAKTHI" and Iran Consular New Delhi

Prof. Puri lighting the lamp on the inauguration ceremony Vedic convention in front of all the spiritual leaders.

Prof. Puri with H. H. Swami Chidanand Saraswati ji President Parmath Nikaten Rishikash.

Prof. Puri with Dr. Yoganand Shastri Minister Health & Social Welfare Govt. Of NCT of Delhi

Sri Sri Ravi Shankar ji, giving blessings to Prof. Puri

Dr. Yoganand Shastri Minister Health & Social Welfare Govt. of NCT of Delhi, H. H. Swami Chidanand Saraswati ji President Parmath Nikaten. Releasing the book written by Prof. Puri

Prof. Puri delivering Key note address at International Vedic Convention , New Delhi

Prof. Puri discussing with Dr. Karan Singh and Shri D.R Kaarthikeyan Ex. CBI Director

Sri Sri Ravi Shankar ji, Presenting the Award to Prof. Puri

Master of Wisdom Award Presented to Prof. Puri by Sri Sri Ravi Shankar ji

ABOUT THE AUTHOR

PROF. BHARAT BHUSHAN PURI

Prof. Dr. B. B. Puri is a multifaceted personality and he is a Senior Practicing Architect, Research Scholar, Author and Vastu Advisor. He is associated with numerous professional organizations. His achievements highlight his versatile character.

Prof. Puri has added a new research dimension and scientific approach to Vedic Culture making it a modern concept. His mission is to propagate the new dimensions in the Vedic Philosophy and get due recognition for it.

Prof. Puri's creative ability has earned him many commendations from Dr. Zakir Hussain, Shri V. V. Giri, Dr. Giani Zail Singh, and Dr. Shankar Dayal Sharma, Shri. K. R. Narayanan, Former Presidents of India. He was also honored with a shield and testimonial by Smt. Indira Gandhi, and Shri. Rajiv Gandhi, Former Prime Ministers of India.

He has traveled widely and has participated in and headed many National and International Conferences and Seminars. He is the recipient of numerous awards and notes of appreciation from renowned personalities. He has been honored with the **Bharat Gaurav Award** (1996), **Bhaskar Award** (1997) **Business Initiative Development Award**

(1998), **The Gem of India Award** (1998), **National Excellency Award** (1999), **Health Excellence Award** (2000), **The International Academician Fellowship Award** (2002). A Biographical note on Prof. Puri was featured in **India's Who's Who Book** (1978) and **Prominent Personalities of India**, (1979). **Master of Wisdom National Award 2008 by Media Trust of India, Vedic Signature award 2008.** On 27th May 2009, the M.G.I & R.T.I. Moka Mauritius, awarded **THE LIGHT OF EAST Award 2009** and **Distinguished Service Award - 2010 by Geriatric Society of India, Lifetime Achievement Award by 2011 World Management Congress (The Global Open University Nagaland)** to Prof. Dr. B. B Puri.

He has been honored with **The Millennium Award** and a Gold Medal at the Millennium World Congress (2000) for his lifetime achievements.

Prof. Puri has written more than 120 books, the then Hon'ble President of India released his popular books titled **'Vedic Architecture & Art of Living'** and **'Applied Vastu Shastra in Modern Architecture'**. His latest book titled **"Vastu Science For 21st Century to Enjoy the Gift of Nature"**. **'The Ageless Mind'**, **'The Art of Blissful Living, Spiritual laws of Vedic Philosophy'**, **'Domestic Herbal remedies'** and **'Life Before Death'** have been well received.

Prof. Puri is the founder & Chairman: -

- Research Institute of Vedic Culture (Trust. N.G.O)
- Vastu Research Centre
- Design Gurukul. (An Institution for Professionals)
- Vastu Kala Academy (College of Architecture)
- The Institution of Vastu Science (India)
- Grover & Puri (Architects & Town Planner, since 1960)
- **Chairman:-** Indian Institute of Building Technology (IIBT)

- Prof. Puri & Associates, Architect & Vastu Adviser
- **Director**, World Academy of Spiritual Sciences (WASS)
- **Head of Occult Science Dept.** Zoroastrian College (Mumbai)
- **Vice President: -** Geriatric society of India
- **Chief Adviser: -** ProGen Nutraceuticals Pvt. Ltd. & R.K. Group Corporation Ltd

Prof. Puri is the Life Member: -

- International Council of Consultants
- Indian Building Congress
- India International Center
- Indian Council of Social Welfare
- Institute of Chartered Engineers
- A.M.I.C.E. India & U.S.A.
- Council of Architecture

Member:-

- India Habitat Center
- Engineering Council of India
- Construction Industry Development Council

Visiting Professor:-

- CPWD Training Institute Govt. of India.
- ALTC Govt. of India.
- Zoroastrian College, Mumbai.
- M.G.I. Moka Mauritius
- Tribhuvan University, Kathmandu, Nepal.

Web: - www.profpurivrc.com

E-mail dr.bbpuri@yahoo.com , dr.bbpuri@hotmail.com

Books Released by V.V.I.P.
Authored by Prof. Dr. B. B. Puri

Prof. Puri Presenting his book to **Shri K. R. Narayanan Former President of India.**

Book Released by **Hon'ble President of India, Shri Shankar Dayal Sharma,** on 3'rd July 1997 at Rashtrapati Bhawan.

Released by **Swami Chinmayanand Ji Minister of State** for Home Affairs on 7th April 2003, at India Habitat Centre

Book released by **Hon'ble President of India, Shri Shankar Dayal Sharma**, on 26th Dec, 1995 at Rashtrapati Bhawan

H. E. the Governor of Bihar, releasing "Mass Scale Housing For Hot Climate" A book on architecture authored by Prof. Dr. B. B. Puri

H.E. Consul General Alexander Mantysky Releasing the Book's Author by Prof. Dr. B. B. Puri, at Russia Cultural Centre in Present of Dame Dr. Prof. Meher Master Moos

Some of the Books written By B. B. Puri

Life Before Death
(Published by MD Publications Pvt. Ltd)

The Art of Bliss full Living
(Published by Motilal Banarsidas Publisers Pvt. Ltd)

Domestic Herbal Remedies
(Published by New Age Books)

A Practical Guide to an Ageless Mind
(Published by Research Institute of Vedic Culture)

Vastu Science for 21st Century, To Enjoy The Gift Of Nature
(Published by New Age Books)

Vedic Architecture & Art of Living
(Published by Vastu Gyan Publication)

Applied Vastu Shastra in Modern Architecture
(Published by Vastu Gyan Publication).

Mass Scale Housing for Hot Climate.
(Published by Oxford & IBH Publishing Co. Pvt. Ltd.)

The Role of Vedic Culture to enjoy Beneficial Living
(Published by Research Institute of Vedic Culture)

Some of The Books Written By Prof. B. B. Puri

Vastu Science
for 21st Century
to enjoy the gift of nature
Prof. B. B. Puri

A Book on
Vastu Shastra
Vedic Architecture
and
Art of Living
Dr. B.B. Puri

APPLIED VASTU SHASTRA
IN
MODERN ARCHITECTURE
BY
PROF. B. B. PURI

Dr. B.B. Puri
Mass Scale
Housing
for
Hot
Climate

Prof. Puri getting the blessings from Late Shri V. V. Giri, the president of India

Shri V. V. Giri, President of India, Presenting Award of Appreciation to Prof. Puri

Shri. Zakir Hussain, the President of India, made the above observation, after inspecting the detailed plans prepared by B. B. Puri. Architect, on the eve of laying the foundation stone of S.G.T.B. Khalsa College, Delhi University.

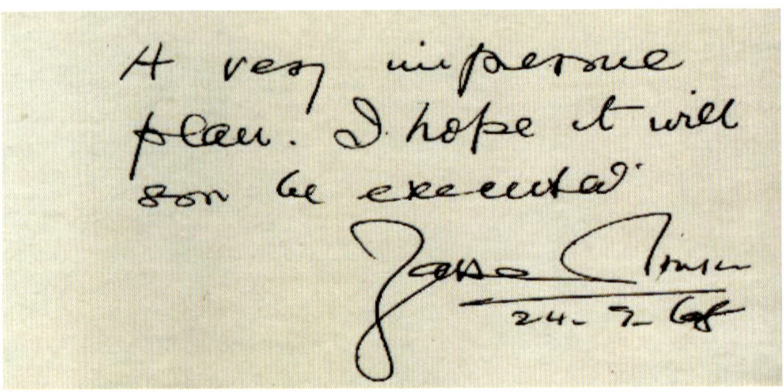

A very impressive plan. I hope it will soon be executed.
24-7-68

Prof. Puri receiving shield of testimonial from Late Smt. Indira Gandhi. Prime Minister of India

Bibliography

Olsborn Alex f. Applied Imagination Principles and Procedure of Creative thinking.

Dr. P.C. Bhalla., The Philosophy of Life.

Swami Chinmayanandji, Taitraya Upanishads.

Rig Veda, Yajur Veda , Sam Veda , Atharva Veda.

A.C. Bhaktivedanta Swami Prabhupada, Books of His Divine Grace., The Bhaktivedanta Book Trust, Mumbai, 1997.

Indian Monuments through the Ages - Indian Society of Engineering Geology.

The Vedic Age, Bhartiya Vidya Bhawan , Mumbai.

Kautilya's Arthashastra.

Swami Chinmayanandji, Tatva Bodh of Adi Shankaracharyaji.

Dr. P.C. Bhalla., Life and Living Ritika & Radhika Publications, New Delhi, 1998.

Prof. Dr. B. B. Puri., Vedic Architecture and Art of Living. Vastu Gyan Pulication, New Delhi, 1998.

Prof. Dr. B. B. Puri., A Practical Guide to an Ageless Mind.,Research Institute of Vedic Culture, New Delhi 2004.

Prof. Dr. B. B. Puri., The Art of Bliss full Living., Motilal Banarsidas Publisers Pvt. Ltd, New Delhi 2008.

Prof. Dr. B. B. Puri., Domestic Herbal Remedies., New Age Books, New Delhi.

Prof Dr B B Puri, Life Before Death, MD Publications Pvt Ltd, New Delhi 2010.

LIFE BEFORE DEATH

ISBN-978-81-7533-314-7

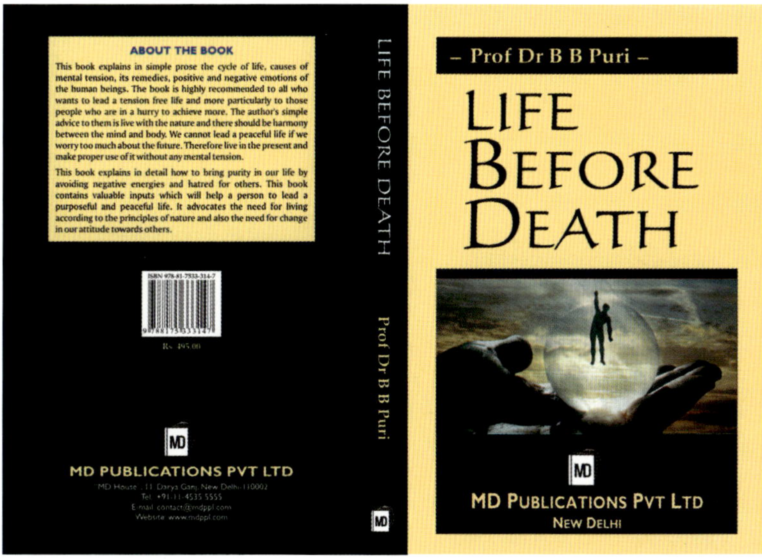

Index

C

D

E

N

O

P

Q

R

S

T